The Teacher's Role

in Counseling

Foundations of Secondary Education
Jean D. Grambs, Editor

The Teacher's Role
in Counseling

MARY G. LIGON and SARAH W. McDANIEL
School of Education, Hofstra University

Prentice-Hall, Inc., Englewood Cliffs, New Jersey

Foreword

"But no one would listen . . ."
"If I could only have talked to my teacher . . ."
"Mr. Brooks is someone who makes you feel safe if you
tell him your problems . . ."

The above comments by secondary school students
are a reflection upon the way teachers do or do not
function adequately in their counseling roles. To the
degree that teachers are able to listen, to accept student
problems realistically, to show sensitivity to students
who wish advice and counsel, are the schools able to
meet the pressures of today's complex world?

Each year secondary schools appear to get larger,
more impersonal, more "institutional." Instead of being
a name, a student is a number. Often he is shuffled
through programs and classes with mechanical effi-
ciency, and sometimes with mechanical error and in-
flexibility.

At this point—in the history of the world as well as

in the history of youth—it seems particularly pressing that each teacher gain skill in human understanding and the range of related skills which are those of the teacher-counselor. These skills are not inherent, just because one is a person of good-will. Counseling skills must be acquired: sensitivity to the hidden messages of others and responding appropriately are behaviours most of us must learn by deliberate effort.

This volume by Doctors Ligon and McDaniel represents a major effort to provide explicit and substantial assistance for the teacher-to-be, and to the experienced teacher as well, in the fundamentals of knowledge and guidance skills every teacher can utilize. The volume is not intended to make "finished" counselors out of classroom teachers. But every day in countless ways teachers do help—or fail to help—their students. This volume is unique in keeping the teacher at the center of discussion. The case material, the suggestions for role playing, the information about referral sources, are all designed with the classroom teacher in mind. The authors bring to the book a rich background as counselors in the classroom and guidance office, and as trainers of counselors and guidance personnel. They know how teachers feel; they know how youth feel; and they know and appreciate the ways adequate bridges of trust and understanding can be built.

Most secondary school educators would agree whole-heartedly with the statements made above. Unfortunately, the typical secondary education preparation provides little room for explicit training in counseling skills. Also, the average textbook used in such programs either ignores the teacher's counseling functions, or treats them very superficially. Thus the Ligon and McDaniel book is designed to make up for this lack, to supplement the standard methods textbook with the kind of practical assistance the classroom teacher can use.

It has been commented that if each student had one teacher, each year, who knew and cared about him, 99% of our troubled youth would no longer be in trouble. It is towards this end that this book is presented.

Jean D. Grambs
University of Maryland

Preface

Perhaps at no other time in the history of this country has there been a greater "generation gap" and at the same time a greater need for close relationships between adults and adolescents. Adolescents face a world which, while exciting and full of change, is frightening and often incomprehensible. Moreover, they feel increasing anonymity and alienation in school situations in particular and life in general. Adolescents need adult help in forming values and developing understandings about themselves that will help them grow toward responsible adulthood, fully aware of who they are and able to face the challenges and uncertainties which are concomitant with the rapid rate of change in today's world. Other than their parents, teachers are the adults with whom they are most in contact.

This book is written for preservice and in-service secondary school teachers. It explains what counseling is and defines the role of school counselor so that teachers can understand this essential resource of the school. It then discusses some of the areas in which students may be looking for help and ways in which teachers can deal effectively with student concerns and problems.

It is committed to the idea that teachers can and do enter into counseling or helping relationships with their students and that students can find in teachers some of the support and courage they need as they approach adult status. Students have always come to teachers for counsel. Teachers therefore need to know how to be most helpful to those students who seek them out for more than help in subject matter. They should know what they can and what they cannot do to help, seeing their counseling as an enrichment of the teaching which remains their prime responsibility.

To say that teachers can and should assume counseling responsibilities does not detract from the role of the school counselor, but rather enhances it. The school counselor's job is made easier by each teacher who is able to establish counseling relationships with his student and to show his student that there are some adults whom he can trust, in whom he can confide, and who honestly care about him as a person. This kind of teacher will be more sensitive to student concern and more likely to make referrals to the school counselor. We do not draw a clear line between the counseling of teachers and that of counselors because we believe that lines must be drawn anew with each situation in accord with the best judgment of those involved. On the whole, teachers' counseling is short-term and related to concerns that stem from the classroom, while counselors spend more time counseling, which is their prime responsibility, and help students deal with a wide range of concerns. The school counselor remains the one who has special skills and who is usually most competent to enter into counseling relationships with students. However, each situation varies with such things as the availability and competence of the school counselor, the competence of the teacher as a counselor, the trust the student feels toward whom, the relationship between teacher and counselor, and the circumstances which precipitate the student's need for counseling.

We wish to thank those many people who have contributed to the writing of this book. Whatever readers find useful and helpful can be attributed in large measure to students and colleagues in high schools where we have taught and counseled and to our counselor education students at Hofstra University. They have provided us with case material, challenged our thinking, and helped us in forming and reforming our ideas. Dr.

Walter Ligon, Dr. Gladys Murphy, and Dr. John Van Buren read all or parts of the manuscript. We are grateful to them for the time, support, and thoughtful criticism they gave so unstintingly. Mrs. Josephine Sadowski cheerfully and accurately typed the entire manuscript. Miss April Ragona, Miss Judith Wiss and Mrs. Adrienne Daly typed parts of it. All of the typists contributed to our morale by enjoying what they typed. Finally, we should like to thank Dr. Jean D. Grambs for her encouragement, patience, and careful editing.

Mary G. Ligon
Sarah W. McDaniel

Contents

Introduction

Susan hesitated outside the door, waiting for Mrs. Howe to see her.

"Hello, Susan. Are you looking for me?"

"Yes, I wanted to talk to you about that long-term assignment you gave us."

Mrs. Howe, always glad to have students stop by to talk about their work, asked Susan to sit down while she finished checking a paper. Susan was a good student with occasional flashes of excellence which suggested she could be more than a good student. Her work at a stopping point, Mrs. Howe turned to Susan to clear up her questions about the assignment. Later, as Susan was gathering up her books preparatory to leaving, Mrs. Howe asked casually about her plans for college. To her amazement tears welled up in Susan's eyes.

"Oh, Mrs. Howe, I don't know. My parents want me to go to one place, I want to go to another. They're completely unreasonable. I can't talk to them. They're on my back all the time to make up my mind their way. I'm not even sure I want to go to college. Richard wants us to get married when he gets out of the army in October."

1

Tears streamed down Susan's face as Mrs. Howe stared at her.

The purpose of this book is to help teachers understand and cope with situations like these. Mrs. Howe's situation is not at all unusual and is based on actual experience. It could be duplicated under varying circumstances almost any time teachers are dealing with individual students. All teachers encounter students who present problems to them either directly as Susan has done or indirectly through their behavior. What should Mrs. Howe do? Listen? Change the subject? Hand her a tissue? Reassure her? Run for the school counselor? Refer her to the school psychologist? Tell her she can't help? Is it part of her responsibility as a teacher to do anything?

This book gives teachers some bases on which to decide what to do, and how to respond to students who in one way or another confront teachers with their problems and concerns. Students' problems, which come with them to their classes, are important to teachers because all too often they interfere with students' ability to profit from classes and hence to learn what teachers are trying to communicate in the educational process of helping students grow toward mature adulthood.

We will offer no formulas or prescriptions to cover all cases. Because we are dealing with human beings, no situation will ever be exactly the same as another. When we think we have encountered everything, we meet something new. However, there is information about counseling and what school counselors do which can help teachers make intelligent, understanding responses when dealing with students as individuals as well as in groups, and which will clarify teachers' responsibilities in handling situations like Mrs. Howe's. Teachers' thoughtful utilization of counseling and guidance approaches can enhance teaching immeasurably by strengthening interpersonal relationships between teachers and their students and can contribute substantially to that teaching which is concerned with the total development of individuals.

PART ONE

Professional Counseling

Teachers, in examining their responsibilities for counseling with students, will find it useful to study the operations of counseling and guidance programs in the schools. It is important for them to know what school counselors can do so that they know what help to expect from them in working with students. Chapter 1 discusses briefly what school counselors do, providing a framework for the description of counseling in Chapter 2. Chapter 3 examines the counseling needs adolescents bring with them into the classroom.

1

The School Counselor

One of the first thoughts Mrs. Howe might have in deciding what to do about Susan would be to talk with her school counselor. In order to make an intelligent decision whether or not to seek the counselor's assistance, she needs to know what the school counselor's role is: what his competencies are, and what help a teacher, student, or parent can expect from him. Based on one's own experience and needs, each person—teacher, student, or parent—tends to see the school counselor differently. Teachers often base their perceptions on their experience, or lack of experience, with particular school counselors whom they have encountered. You might find it helpful to recall your own experiences with school counselors and compare them with the experiences of your friends.

A school counselor may be seen primarily as a Giver of Tests. "All he does is sit in his office and give tests."

Or a College Broker. "He sure recommended the wrong college to my kid."

Or a Crying Towel. "He lets the kids cry on his shoulder all the time about how awful their teachers are."

5

Or an Advice Giver. "The counselor will advise you about the best courses to take."

Or a Sympathetic Listener. "If it hadn't been for my counselor in high school, I'd never have made it."

A Profession Coming of Age

Ask a group of teachers to list things that school counselors do and you will have a list with as many as 100 different activities. All these views may have some truth in them. Our task is to draw together more accurate descriptions of the school counselor so that teachers will better understand his many contributions to the educational process.

That school counselors are seen so differently is not surprising. Different school counselors do indeed behave differently from one another, giving various degrees of emphasis to different activities. Some variation is not only legitimate but necessary, for schools, like people, have different needs. The history of the development of guidance and counseling also explains some of the variations. The field has responded to different needs such as those for moral guidance, better occupational choice, more individual attention to students as schools grew larger, and changing curriculum and grouping with the increasingly heterogeneous population of secondary schools. These needs have developed along with increasing population, scientific and technological advances, and now automation. In response to these different pressures, guidance and counseling has developed somewhat haphazardly, with insufficient rationale. However, it is now coming of age.

School counseling is in the midst of becoming a specialized profession within the profession of education. Recognizing the confusion surrounding school counseling, The American Personnel and Guidance Association has over the past few years done an outstanding job of defining the role and preparation of the school counselor. Rather than let other people say what they should do, school counselors are taking a hand in defining their own role. This has been an exciting and demanding undertaking which is sure to result in better understanding of what counselors are for and a higher level of operation on the part of school counselors.

Ideas of what school counselors should do are changing and will doubtless, in these fast-moving times, continue to change.

One indication of change is the trend to call guidance counselors *school counselors* because the word *guidance* is loaded with connotations of manipulation and direction. Although the label used does not seem important to us, we choose to use the title *school counselor* because the professional organization, a division of the American Personnel and Guidance Association, is the American School Counselor Association.

Other and more exciting changes will come with increased use of computers and information retrieval systems, with different ideas about the best ways of counseling educationally disadvantaged students, and with new modes of teaching. For example, computers are already being programmed for counseling students in planning their high school programs.[1] Information retrieval systems will be used increasingly to help school counselors and their students keep up with occupational and educational information. New ways of working with groups will enable school counselors to work with more students. Byrne sees the counselor of the future as a full professional ". . . who functions in ways so as to accelerate the learning and general development of all students, and helps assess and improve the school's climate for mental health."[2] This future professional will be supported by technicians who will perform many of the tasks, which school counselors currently perform, which call for less training than a professional counselor requires.

The American Personnel and Guidance Association gives a clear statement of counselor role and recommendations for counselor education to which teachers can refer.[3] We propose to discuss what a school counselor does a little differently so that we can occasionally refer back to the case in the Introduction where Mrs. Howe asked Susan about her college plans and was greeted with a tearful response.

Guidance is the over-all term commonly applied to the activities of a school counselor. Counseling is one of the activities which this term encompasses. School counselors perform other activities which are not counseling but which are legitimately part of their

[1] J. F. Cogswell, C. P. Donahoe, Jr., B. P. Estaven, and B. A. Rosenquist, "The Design of a Man-Machine Counseling System." Paper presented at the American Psychological Association Convention, September 4, 1966, New York.

[2] Richard Hill Byrne, "High School Counseling—Conditions for Change," *Guidance-Personnel Work: Future Tense*, ed. Margaret Ruth Smith (New York: Teachers College Press, 1966), p. 43.

[3] John W. Loughary, ed., *Counseling, A Growing Profession* (Washington, D.C.: American Personnel and Guidance Association, 1965), pp. 93–106.

role in assisting students to gain as much as possible from their school experience. Guidance, where it exists, is sometimes a separate department. In large school systems, it is often placed in a department of pupil personnel services along with school psychologists, school social workers, school nurse teachers, attendance teachers, and sometimes reading specialists. The organizational structure differs from school district to school district. Some districts have all these pupil personnel services directly available to those within the district. Others have services available on a county-wide basis. Still others serve such sparsely populated areas that few if any of these services are available to them, though mobile counseling units are beginning to be used.

What School Counselors Can Do

Within the framework of guidance and pupil personnel services, we shall be talking about what a school counselor's competencies are—what he *can* do, not necessarily what he *does* do. It would be nice if what he *can* do and what he *does* do were more often the same. Unfortunately, school counselors are not always able to perform as effectively as one would wish. Of course, this holds true for other members of the school community as well. Teachers are often frustrated because large classes or a restrictive curriculum prevent them from doing all they would like to. Administrators can be equally frustrated by things like limited budgets or recalcitrant school boards. In the case of school counselors, the reasons for the difference between what is and what ought to be are varied. Often, public expectations focus so strongly on pre-college counseling that counselors are pressed to spend most of their time on college-bound students although their competencies should be available to *all* students. Administrators and teachers sometimes do not understand what counselors can do and hence do not use them effectively or, on the other hand, expect a kind of instant solution to student problems which is not possible. The bureaucracy of the school is sometimes not friendly to counselors, whose focus is on the individual. Counselors themselves are often not committed enough to stand against the pressures which work against their doing a good job.

The pressures on school counselors are tremendous. In suburban and some urban schools, they are expected to place each student not only in college but preferably in the college of his first choice, and their effectiveness is judged by the percentage of college acceptances even though precollege counseling is but one part of their job. In ghetto areas, school counselors are faced with unbelievably high case loads of students who are most in need of the individual concern and care which counselors can offer them. Urban problems of housing, poverty, unemployment, and racial tension are reflected in pressures on school counselors as well as on teachers in these schools. Counselors in all schools are beset by students, teachers, parents, and administrators asking for solutions to problems. It takes a competent, committed school counselor to develop and maintain his role as he thinks it ought to be.

In school counseling, the increased activity of professional organizations combined with changes in counselor education is contributing to better functioning of school counselors. Statements from the professional organizations recommend two years of broad and rigorous graduate study for counselors. More schools are beginning to ask school counselors to do more than read college catalogs and persuade students to study harder.

We are well aware that many guidance and counseling programs do not function as they are described in textbooks, but we are convinced that they *can* function that way and that schools need strong guidance and counseling programs. Teachers can benefit by knowing what is possible and can even help school counselors work toward stronger programs by supporting demands for lighter student loads, more clerical help, or whatever is needed in the particular school to produce an effective guidance and counseling program.

Commitment   School counselors are committed to the best interests of the individual within the system. Leo Goldman has said that they stand as ". . . the school's conscience concerning the individual."[4] They keep the focus on what is best for Jim or Susan. As a teacher, Mrs. Howe must be concerned with the groups which she teaches; in deciding what to do about Susan, she must consider the effects of her decision on her classes. The counselor is there to direct concern toward Susan alone. Concern for both the group and the individual is, of course, important. The welfare of each is dependent in some measure on the other.

[4]Leo Goldman, "The Individual in Guidance—A Paradox." Paper presented at the annual conference of the New York State Counselors Association, March 20, 1965, New York.

But the counselor's commitment is to the individual. He is committed, also, to belief in what school counseling can contribute to the educational process, to the education and development of Susan, just as teachers are committed to the value of the subject matter they are teaching to adolescents. School counselors see themselves as contributing to the school as counselors, consultants, and coordinators.

Counseling   Mrs. Howe might suggest to Susan that she go see her counselor. If Susan did—and it ought to be up to her whether or not she goes—she would meet an adult skilled in communicating with adolescents. The school counselor knows how to form a relationship with a student where the student can express his hopes, concerns, and puzzlements with freedom from fear or ridicule. Lucky student! Not many of us have an opportunity like this. He has freedom of communication without the responsibility of conforming to the standards of the counselor. He has the freedom to bring all that he is and all that he has learned to a focus. This does not mean that Mrs. Howe is left out. Part of what Susan has learned and will learn comes from her teachers. She learns about herself from the way teachers behave toward her. But in the counseling relationship, Susan is free to be just what she is. She does not have to worry about grades or judgments. She can talk about her plans for the future, her feelings about her parents, or her mixed feelings about marriage without fear of ridicule or even good advice. And in this situation, she may be able to begin to see answers for herself. Some counselors will tell her what they think might be best. Others will let Susan take the lead during the counseling. All good counselors will let Susan make her own decisions and respect her for them even if they do not agree.

There is, of course, much more to counseling than this, but later chapters will dwell at length on what counseling is, what the counseling relationship is like, and the kinds of counseling in which teachers are likely to engage.

The benefit of counseling for Susan is that she will be able to carry out her developmental tasks and learn the process of decision making. No one will be making a decision for her; she will be learning to make her own. The opportunity for this kind of experience is part of the educational process, not an extra service or a frill. In addition, as Susan is able to work out some of her concerns, she may be free to use her abilities more effectively in her chosen direction. She will be more free to become what she wants to and can become.

The counselor's insistence that Susan is free to make her own decisions may lead him into conflict with others in the school who might feel, for example, that the counselor should persuade Susan to go on to college rather than to consider marriage. The counselor, however, is one person who does not persuade, cajole, coax, or admonish. He respects Susan enough as an individual to allow her to choose her own direction. He may help her see alternatives and consequences and provide her with necessary information, but in the end the decision is hers. This is part of his commitment to the individual.

Consulting   Because of his knowledge of adolescent behavior, his awareness from listening to students of the impact of the school on them, and his familiarity with patterns of educational and vocational development, the school counselor is competent to serve as consultant to adults who deal with students on a significant basis. Adults—parents, teachers, administrators—are sometimes puzzled by the actions of adolescents. They are concerned about unexpected changes in behavior. They feel the need to talk things over with someone who is competent in adolescent psychology and styles of learning. The school counselor can, if called upon, help parents and teachers to understand better the meaning of adolescents' actions. He can act as consultant to individuals or to groups of interested adults.

Mrs. Howe might want to talk with Susan's counselor so that she can better understand Susan, the kinds of problems she is facing, and the relationship of these problems to Susan's school work and her responsibility as Susan's teacher. Mrs. Howe and the counselor together might discuss the possibliities open to Mrs. Howe, although not even the counselor can tell her what to say or how to react to Susan right now as she is in her room crying. But if Mrs. Howe has talked with the counselor before and knows something of how she can help, it will give her a little something to go on at this crucial point.

If the counselor and Mrs. Howe decide that Mrs. Howe should counsel with Susan if Susan so desires, then the counselor is there to serve as a consultant to Mrs. Howe in her counseling endeavors, to talk over with her what goes on in her counseling sessions. If they decide that Susan might be helped by seeing the counselor, then the counselor can help Mrs. Howe know how to refer Susan to him. And, most important, counselor and teacher together can often work out ways of changing the classroom situation to help individual students such as Susan.

Parents are sometimes puzzled by the behavior of their adolescent children, They are also puzzled by some of the things that go on in the schools. They are far removed from the classroom themselves and have little immediate background on which to draw for understanding the demands made by the school. This puzzlement may be particularly prevalent among parents of disadvantaged youths whose own experiences with school were often neither pleasant nor successful. Foreign-born parents have special difficulties. However, all parents encounter some perplexity because what is being taught today is so different from what they were taught. At other times, the demands which parents make on the school need examination in the light of what we know about adolescent development. Here again the counselor can offer consultative services, interpreting the parents to the school and the school to the parents, serving as a mediator in case of conflicting demands.

Following talks with Mrs. Howe or Susan, the counselor may well have occasion to talk with Susan's parents. He would want to use his knowledge of adolescent behavior to help them understand and accept Susan. They could expect him to offer them both his counseling and consulting skills during what is probably a difficult time for them, to help them work with Susan in the decisions that *she* has to make.

The counselor's commitment is to foster practices which help the adolescent best accomplish the things he has to do in order to become the person that only he can become. Uncommitted to specific curricular or educational practices, the counselor can sometimes bring a different viewpoint to the resolution of behavioral and learning problems.

The school counselor is also a consultant for different kinds of information needed to help students progress smoothly through school and to make decisions for their future. He is responsible for gathering information about students and seeing that it is accessible to teachers—information which can help teachers teach more effectively. Such information may include data about relevant family background, health, past achievement, present ability as indicated by standardized tests, and comments by other teachers. He not only gathers the information but also helps teachers interpret the information and know how to use it in the class-room.

The counselor's office is also a source of occupational and college information. Contrary to what is often the public's expectation, the school counselor cannot know all about more than 1,900 colleges and 40,000 changing occupations. Students and parents, however, can expect him to have much of the information available in occupational files and college reference books and to know where to find other information. New ways of storing and conveying these kinds of information are in the experimental stage. Computers which students can ask for specific information and receive TV screen, filmstrip, or printout responses are being used experimentally. Devices such as these are needed to keep up with the rapidly changing occupational and employment picture.

Coordinating   Perhaps Susan needs other kinds of help than those the counselor offers directly, that is, she may need psychological help or perhaps has some health problems. By studying Susan, the counselor can learn what kinds of things she needs from the school. He knows what services are available in the school and community for adolescents and their families. As coordinator, the counselor has skill in bringing together the parent and/or student with the required services. He would do more than send Susan to a helping resource. He would help her to be receptive to the specialized help that she needs.

The quantity and quality of helping services vary tremendously, of course, from school to school. Schools in rural districts are often served by county or regional facilities. Some large schools have so many special services within the school that teachers are uncertain to which specialist to refer a student should the occasion arise. As a result, the same student is sometimes referred to different services by different teachers without one specialist knowing that the other is working with the same student. The counselor serves to coordinate the different services. He is knowledgable about what facilities there are and how they can best be used. Of necessity, he must be skilled in human relations in order to assist personnel from many disciplines to work together for the good of a particular child. He is *not* skilled in all areas of individual service. He *is* the person who receives a student at the beginning of any difficulty and then utilizes and coordinates the resources of the school and community to help that child.

How They Work

Thus far we have talked about what a school counselor is competent to do: counsel, consult, and coordinate. In addition, a school counselor works in less obvious ways. One might say that he has certain strategies. These strategies stem from what he does as counselor, coordinator, and consultant, and are necessary to his effective functioning.

Initiating Change   As a school counselor listens to students, consults with teachers, and coordinates the resources of the school to help individual students, he often is made aware of things in the school which need change if the best interests of individual students are to be served. Sometimes he sees practices which are actually inimical to individual development. If he counsels with Susan, perhaps Susan will help him see that academic competition in his school and pressure to attend college are so strong that she is unable to function as well as she could. Listening to other students and teachers, he may learn that the school's curriculum is particularly limited for students of low ability. His commitment is to the individual student—to Susan. If his commitment is real, he *must* try to change those situations in the school which he sees as damaging or limiting to individual students. He cannot bring about change singlehandedly, for he is not competent in all phases of the school's operations. But he can bring harmful practices to the attention of the appropriate people in the school and he can suggest change. He can also keep working for change.

The image of the school counselor as an active innovator is new. He has not usually been seen as such nor seen himself as such. As it has become increasingly clear that he *must* be an innovator to do what he wants to do as counselor and as it has become clear that he is ideally located in the school to know what is going on, he has begun to accept the role of initiator of change. Stewart and Warnath base their book on the notion of a school counselor who

> . . . attempts to promote a type of society that is hospitable to youth—a society that provides students ample

opportunity and encouragement to become self-directing, purposeful, productive adults. Perhaps it is by promoting such an environment that the counselor can be most effective in attaining his goals.[5]

Facilitating Communication and Mediating   The school counselor's competencies are used to facilitate communication among those concerned with the education of students where failures in communications are hindering the educational process. His skill in listening to people makes it possible for him to interpret one person to another—principal to teacher, parent to child, child to teacher—so that they are better able to communicate with each other. He may interpret Susan's parents to her so that she can talk more easily to them about her feelings. He may help a principal understand the teacher's anxieties precipitated by an administrative bulletin. His purpose is to enhance freer communication, not to take it over. He is a catalyst in the communicative process within the school.

In much the same way, the school counselor may mediate between people where understanding has broken down. Students are pressured by so many—parents, teachers, adults in general. Often, he may try to protect a student from these pressures so that the student can take time to think about what *he* wants and who *he* is. He may be more than a mediator and become an advocate for the student when he thinks that the odds are heavy against him. He may mediate between parent and school, school and community, or student and societal demands.

In these strategies, the counseling, consulting, and coordinating skills of a school counselor culminate. He gives unique service to the educational process.

Counselors and Teachers Depend on Each Other

A school counselor who cannot get along with teachers is not likely to be of much use in a school. He alone is responsible for what goes on in the one-to-one relationship which is counseling, but he depends on what are called the *significant others*, that is, teachers, parents, and others who are important in a student's life, for much of what he wants to do outside the counseling relationship. If Susan needs counseling help, she may also need

[5]L. H. Stewart and C. F. Warnath, *The Counselor and Society: A Cultural Approach* (Boston: Houghton Mifflin Company, 1963), p. 11.

help and understanding from others who are important to her. The counselor must be trusted and liked if he is to interpret Susan to these others. Mrs. Howe will not even consult the counselor about Susan unless she trusts him. Susan is unlikely to come to the counselor on her own initiative unless she senses from others that he is a person who can help her. His effectiveness in helping individual students is severely limited unless others in the school trust, respect, and like him. His relationship with teachers, who see much more of students than he does, is particularly crucial.

Unfortunately, there is sometimes hostility between counselors and teachers, often deriving from misunderstanding and poor communication. Each side needs to understand the contribution of the other to its work. So much advantage for students can be gained by working together that it is a shame to allow anything to stand in the way. Teachers can help minimize misunderstanding by making it their business to become acquainted with the counselors in the school.

What Teachers Can Expect from the School Counselor   We have described what a counselor does in broad terms. What we want to do now is to describe some of the things he does while he counsels, consults, and coordinates which can be helpful to teachers. To do this, let's look again at Mrs. Howe in her room with the weeping Susan. What can she expect from the school counselor?

At this very moment, she cannot expect anything. She is the only one there with Susan. She is talking with her. She must respond. There is no one else who can tell her what to say right then and there. If she knows something about counseling adolescents, she will have some idea of how to respond. She can expect a school counselor to help her learn about counseling within the limits of her teaching responsibility.

When Susan is settled enough to leave for the day, Mrs. Howe can expect the counselor to be a consultant to her in deciding what more to do, if anything, and to consider the various alternatives. As the person who is responsible for testing programs and cumulative records, the school counselor can bring more information to bear on the decision. He can help Mrs. Howe understand Susan's test scores, her previous grades, teacher comments, etc. He cannot tell Mrs. Howe exactly what to do. That is Mrs. Howe's decision. He cannot remove responsibility for Susan from her because Susan will continue to be in class. He can, however, share responsibility.

Even if Susan goes to the counselor for counseling, she will remain in Mrs. Howe's class and will probably want to talk with her from time to time. She trusts her or she would not have confided in her as she did. The more adults she can trust, the better, so the counselor will not want to do anything to take Susan away from Mrs. Howe. On the contrary, he will want to encourage this good relationship even if he himself establishes a counseling relationship with Susan. Mrs. Howe can expect that counseling with the school counselor may help Susan know how to handle her problems better. It may not change her class work. With a better understanding of the pressures on her, Susan might even decide to spend less time studying and more time playing. Though counseling often results in improved class work and behavior, Mrs. Howe cannot expect it. The school counselor is interested in what is best for Susan. School might not be the most important thing for her at this time. Mrs. Howe certainly cannot expect a spectacular change of any kind as the result of one or two interviews.

Mrs. Howe can also expect help with Susan's parents, either in talking with them herself should they come to school or in referring them to the counselor. The counselor can help Mrs. Howe understand the parents and he can help the parents understand Susan.

Teachers can expect school counselors, then, to help them know more about their students so that they can talk with them with more understanding as well as teach them with more understanding. Test results are often so misused that they are more damaging than useful to students. Counselors are there to interpret test scores so that teachers know what the scores tell about students and to help them use test results more intelligently. They may share other information with teachers, as professional colleagues, that will help them teach more effectively. Although students' cumulative records should be easily available, counselors can review them with teachers so that they learn as much as possible from them.

Teachers cannot expect school counselors to share information which is given them in confidence by parents, students, or any other person. Teachers sometimes find this insistence on confidentiality irritating, but it means teachers too can confide in counselors without fear that they will relay what has been said to the principal, other colleagues, parents, or students.

Teachers cannot expect school counselors to have instant success. They will not see immediate changes in students who are counseled. Counselors cannot give pat answers to problems with students. They can help teachers learn how to deal with students like Susan but will not remove problems from their ken. Students in the classroom are the teachers' responsibility.

School counselors will listen to what teachers have to say and work with them to bring about change in situations which both agree are detrimental to good education. But they cannot and typically will not try to make immediate changes for teachers nor intercede with the administration.

Because counseling means listening to students and accepting what they have to say, school counselors hear complaints about teachers from time to time. They are interested in understanding how students see the school so they listen. Listening does not mean agreeing. They will not make judgments about teachers on the basis of what they hear in counseling nor will they betray the confidence of students by passing it on to others. Later chapters on counseling will discuss problems of listening, acceptance, and confidentiality more fully.

If there is any question of whose side school counselors are on, you can expect them to be on the side of the student. Ideally, they mediate between student and school where there is conflict. In practice, they may throw in on the side of the student because the odds are so heavy on the other side. Teachers, parents, and administrators join forces to persuade a student to a particular course of action or mode of behavior. Counselors are pledged to help students learn how to make their own decisions. They may agree with the others that a particular course of action might be best for a student, but will defend the student's right to choose a different course.

What School Counselors Expect of Teachers   First of all, school counselors expect teachers to have some notion of what services they offer. Unfortunately, many teachers are unsure of the contributions of not only school counselors but also school psychologists and social workers. Teachers in this situation can talk with the counselor about what he does.

Teachers see much more of students than do counselors. The school counselor, therefore, expects teachers to notice students who seem to have counseling needs and refer them to him. He may ask teachers to observe a particular youngster with whom he has been counseling, or he may ask a teacher to take part in a case conference where all the teachers concerned with a youngster discuss ways of helping him. He relies on teachers to provide information about all students for their cumulative records. In helping individual students, the counselor depends on the teacher for much that he does because the teacher is the person who sees students daily in his usual school activities. He expects teachers to be professional colleagues with whom he can talk about students in confidence without fear of teachers' room gossip.

Above all, the counselor expects teachers to like students. His concern is not so much what teachers teach them or whether they keep them quiet as whether they are deeply concerned for their welfare. Of course teachers will teach them and keep them quiet. But he wants teachers to see those who need help, reach out to those who are lost, understand those who give trouble. And in this work, he will give his professional services to teachers.

SUMMARY

School counselors are trained to counsel, consult, and coordinate. To support and enhance these activities, they initiate change, mediate, and facilitate communication. This is what they *can* do. Counselors are not always able to do all these things because of limitations in their competencies or in the school situation. School counselors are commited to the best interests of the individual in the educational process. Knowing what counselors *can* do, teachers can receive a great deal of help from them if they have questions concerning individual students.

SUGGESTED READINGS

Arbuckle, Dugald S., *Pupil Personnel Services in the Modern School*. Boston: Allyn & Bacon, Inc., 1966.
A clear description of pupil personnel services in the American school and of the activities of members of the pupil personnel team—school counselor, school social worker, and school psychologist.

Boy, Angelo V., and Gerald J. Pine, *The Counselor in the Schools: A Reconceptualization.* Boston: Houghton Mifflin Company, 1968.
A soundly based discussion of the school counselor as he can be if he continues to work toward being a truly professional counselor.

Byrne, Richard H., *The School Counselor.* Boston: Houghton Mifflin Company, 1963.
A provocative book with the unusual view that only schools which are ready for school counselors should have them.

Kushel, Gerald, *Discord in Teacher-Counselor Relations.* Englewood Cliffs, N.J.: Prentice-Hall, Inc., 1967.
Case studies from the teacher's point of view which make for interesting and illuminating reading.

Stewart, Lawrence H., and Charles F. Warnath, *The Counselor and Society: A Cultural Approach.* Boston: Houghton Mifflin Company, 1965.
A refreshing book which presents the counselor as a real person concerned with the individual and prepared to change situations which keep the individual from being himself.

Wrenn, Gilbert H., *The Counselor in a Changing World.* Washington, D.C.: American Personnel and Guidance Association, 1962.
Written in order to project some of the changes in the world that would affect what counselors do, it remains in the forefront of thinking about guidance and counseling.

2

What Is Counseling?

Teachers should understand what takes place when their students are in a counseling situation, and what some of the problems are in school counseling. Teachers should also understand counseling because they themselves are often engaged in students' concerns in such a way that an understanding of counseling will help them to know how to help students with those concerns. It is not possible for a teacher to maintain all his relationships with students at the teaching level. The relationship can shift suddenly. For example, a teacher helping a girl after school noticed that she was not paying attention as she usually did.

> What's the matter, Marilyn? You don't seem interested today.

> Oh, Mr. McIntosh, I'm pregnant.

The teacher's innocent question released the worry that Marilyn had had on her mind for days. You who are reading this might like to stop and discuss or think about how you would have responded to Marilyn. What is the first thing you would say. Why? What would you be trying to do?

In the previous chapter, counseling was described as but one portion of the school counselor's work. It is often referred to as the heart of the guidance program and given emphasis as the most important thing that school counselors do, as implied by the title, "School Counselor." We agree that it is the one most important thing that a school counselor does. He uses his counseling skills not only while counseling students, but also in his consultative and coordinative activities. The amount of time particular counselors spend directly counseling students varies with the needs and purposes of the schools in which they work. However, all school counselors spend a sizable portion of their time counseling. If not, they ought not be given the title.

In the literature, counseling is defined in various ways. Shertzer and Stone say that counseling ". . . is an interaction process which facilitates meaningful understanding of self and environment and results in the establishment and/or clarification of goals and values for future behavior."[1] Arbuckle says, "Counseling is not helping the client either to adjust to society or to fight it. It is helping him to come to see who he really is, and what he has and what he does not have; what he can do easily, what he can do with difficulty, and what he probably cannot do at all."[2] Tyler summarizes a discussion of the definition of counseling by saying that ". . . the purpose of counseling is to facilitate wise choices of the sort on which the person's later development depends."[3]

Counseling does not lend itself to easy definition. Intellectual comprehension of counseling is easy enough to gain, but real understanding comes harder with continued reading, study, and first-hand experience. A student of counseling can write a perfect description of counseling but show in practice that he does not really understand what he has written. He may know, for example, that listening is essential to good counseling, yet not himself hear what a counselee is saying to him. He must think and work hard in order to internalize what he is learning about counseling, to make it part of himself. Nor is counseling some-

[1]Bruce Shertzer and Shelley C. Stone, *Fundamentals of Counseling* (Boston: Houghton Mifflin Company, 1968), p. 26.
[2]Dugald Arbuckle, *Counseling: Philosophy, Theory, and Practice* (Boston. Allyn & Bacon, Inc., 1965), p. 44.
[3]Leona Tyler, *The Work of the Counselor*, 3rd ed. (New York: Appleton-Century-Crofts, 1969), p. 13.

thing that can be learned once and for all. The more one counsels, the more one learns about counseling, including the discovery that he really knows very little. Anything as engaged in the human situation as is counseling remains complex and elusive—but fascinating. The more a person reads, thinks, and tries to apply some of the concepts, the closer he will come to appreciating and understanding counseling. Before giving a definition of counseling which we find useful, we should like you to read the following excerpt from a counseling session.

EXAMPLE

As you read this excerpt of a counseling session, think about what the counselor is trying to do. Why does he respond as he does? What attitudes toward people do his responses suggest? How do you think the student responds? Do you like the way the counselor is counseling? Does it seem successful to you? Why?

Jane is a high school senior who has asked to see her counselor.

Counselor: How have you been, Jane?

Jane: Well, I wanted to come by and see you because I've been a little bit worried lately. You know I got my mid-term grades just about a week ago, and I'm not making very good marks anymore. I'm not doing near as well as I did last year and yet I work all the time. It seems like I'm studying harder and working longer than I did last year. I just don't know what to do about it.

Counselor: Your marks aren't as good as last year even though you're spending even more time than you used to, is that it?

Jane: That's right. Of course, I guess I'm taking a pretty hard schedule because I've got six subjects but I had to do this because, you know, I wanted to go to Oakland College next year, and my whole family is worried about me, because I'm not doing so good.

Counselor: This falling off of your grades has everybody pretty worried?

Jane: Yes, and I hate to be a worry to my family right now because I know my mother has a lot of worries and, of course, my grandmother didn't like it very well when

I decided to go to Oakland instead of Central College, because they think I just want to go there to stay near Joe. But that isn't really so. I don't like it up at Central and, besides that, I'm so worried about my mother this year so I thought I'd better, you know, stay around where I could maybe help out if I needed to, but then I make all these changes in my plans and just look at what I'm doing—I'm—well, I'm making *C*'s and *B*'s and I never have done that before.

Counselor: You really want to help out at home but deciding to stay here for college—isn't helping much?

Jane: Well, I think maybe it has helped some. Mother says she can depend on me a good bit but, you see, I'm worried about what is going to happen to me because I'm a senior and I still don't know what I want to do. My aunt keeps telling me, you know, and she keeps kind of pushing. She says I don't have to make up my mind but, every time she comes around she, she, you know, kind of sits down and talks with me about what I'm going to do, and courses I'm going to take in college. They all expect me, you know, to make real good grades because, well, I guess they all, you know, everybody always thought I was—well, real smart ever since I was—well, I think it all goes back to the time that I, you know, I learned to read before I went to school and I never did quite get over that. Maybe my family did and they all thought I was smart and I ought to do real well in school and, you know, I just don't think I'm smart at all. I think everybody has always been mistaken about me, and certainly the grades I'm making now, you wouldn't think anybody who was smart would do that.

Counselor: You said a whole lot there. It sounds as if, maybe it's more than just your grades that are worrying you. You're wondering whether you're as smart as everybody always thought you were. You're not quite sure what direction you want to take.

Jane: Well, I just don't know what I want to do because—well, for awhile I thought I might like to be a nurse but I don't know whether I can really do anything like that or not and, of course, I've always been interested in biology. Ever since I was a little girl, I've been interested in insects and things like that and I did very well in biology, so my aunt and I decided that maybe

I'd better major in some kind of science and that's one trouble because I've got this chemistry course and it takes about—oh, it takes me so much longer to do the experiments than anybody else and it just looks like I spend hours and hours. Maybe I just don't know how to study, I don't know, but I study an awful long time.

Counselor: You spend a lot of time on your studying?

Jane: I work most of the time when I'm not in school. And it bothers me, too, because it looks like I don't have time to do some of the things I really want to do and well, I just don't know—I guess I'm scared because if I keep on—if I made *A*'s and *B*'s last year, I'm making *C*'s this year, looks like I'm just going down.

Counselor: It's getting so bad now, you're not even sure you'll be able to make it in college?

Jane: Well, you know, I guess I didn't want much to go to college in the first place. I talked about not wanting to go to college and, oh, my family just got up in arms 'cause, see, everybody in my family has always been to college and, besides that, they think I'm smart but I just hate to study. Sometimes, when I think about having to go through four more years of this, I just feel like giving up.

Counselor: Then, are you saying maybe you really don't want to go to college?

Jane: I wish . . . I wish there was some way to, you know, for the family to like what I did and yet for me to do something that I really want to do. I don't know what I really want to do. I mean, you know, there are a lot of things. Of course, I don't want to just be a clerk in a store or anything like that but, you know, what I really wished I could do, I think, . . . I think I'd like to well, I think I'd like to take one of these courses in art. I don't mean to go to college and take it. I just don't want any more—I just, of course, know I have to go to college but if you just didn't have so much studying to do.

Counselor: If you could really do what you wanted to do, you would want to go to art school?

Jane: Yes, if I didn't have to go so far away from home. Looks like, you know, all the art schools are away up somewhere away from home and I, I kind of, I guess I'd

be kind of afraid to go away from home, you know, so
far away.

Counselor: You would like to go but it seems like a long
ways away. And then, I guess, you were saying earlier
too, that you're not sure your family would approve.
You sort of feel you ought to do something that they
would like you for.

As we continue to discuss counseling, we hope you will begin
to find answers to those questions asked prior to the counseling
excerpt.

Counseling Defined

Counseling is an encounter in which the counselor helps the
counselee begin to work out the problems or concerns which he
brings with him to the encounter. The goal is to help the counselee arrive at solutions, answers, plans, decisions, or understandings which are satisfactory *to him* and which help him
"become" or grow toward the person that he can be—an independent, self-directing person able to function optimally in the
society in which he lives. We say *begin* to work out because the
problems and concerns brought to counseling are always related
to other problems, concerns, and experiences which may be
worked out later in different situations and at different levels.
The process is not always smooth or easy. It demands self-examination and change by both parties. We all tend to resist change
because it means changes in our habits, routines, and way of
life and these things are tied to our sense of who we are. Therefore the process is often marked with discomfort, discouragement, and backsliding. On the other hand, both parties may find
great satisfaction and growth in the process of counseling.

The range of problems or concerns which a counselee brings
to the encounter is limitless, from life-and-death questions to
immediate decisions about college choices or vocational decisions.

Why should I live?
Should I get a divorce?
Why does my son act this way?
I'm not sure I want to be a teacher after all.
Where can I get a summer job?
Can I succeed in college?

My parents won't listen to me.
How much math do I need?

Each of these concerns or problems may have a range too. The person asking why he should live may be an adult considering suicide or an adolescent pondering life in general. The statement, "I'm not sure I want to be a teacher after all," may reflect clarification of interest, rebellion against parents, or lack of confidence. A question about college requirements may be a simple request for information or an introduction to deeper concern about feelings of inadequacy.

Some of these concerns are likely to come to a school counselor, others are more likely to be heard in a psychologist's or psychiatrist's office. However, a counselor never knows what concerns may be brought to him nor how deep or extensive they may be. To distinguish sharply between counseling and psychotherapy on the basis of the depth of the problem is difficult because there are no clear lines between normal and disturbed, between deep concerns and less deep concerns. In general, psychotherapy deals with the "abnormal" population and counseling with the "normal" population. Psychotherapy typically covers a longer time span than does counseling.

The way counselors deal with the concerns brought to them varies in accord with the particular counseling approach they have developed for themselves. There are many different schools of thought in the field of counseling. Not all counselors would respond in the same way to a statement such as, "I'm not sure I want to go to college." Some possible responses are:

You're not sure college is for you.
What else have you thought about?
Why not?
You're wondering if college is really what you want.
What *do* you want?
Could you tell me more about what you've been thinking?

If the counselee went on to say, "I don't think I have the ability," different responses might be:

You're not sure you could make it.
What kind of grades have you been getting?
Would you like to take some tests and see what they say
    about your ability to succeed in college?
Why do you say that?

Counselors respond in the fashion which seems most appropriate to their own counseling approach. No one approach is any better than another. The counselor, not the approach, is important.

Different People Counsel Differently

Counseling approaches seem to be proliferating and at the same time to be finding more areas of agreement. A few years ago, counselors argued vehemently over the two approaches of directive counseling and nondirective counseling. This controversy seems to have died out though the terms are still in common enough use that we will define them later along with other approaches. With the development of other approaches, discussion has been broadened and also enlightened as experimental studies make more sound data available.

The scope of this book does not allow for discussion of all the counseling approaches nor even adequate discussion of a few. In the list of references there is an entire book devoted to theories of counseling and yet even this book cannot cover all of them.[4] To give some idea of the differences, discussion of areas of disagreement and agreement is followed by brief statements about some of the approaches most likely to be used in school counseling.

Areas of Disagreement   Different counseling approaches are based either implicitly or explicitly on different notions about the nature and behavior of man. Following Allport, Patterson sees essentially two models of man.[5] The first model is that of a reactive being, reacting to either outside forces and stimuli or to his innate needs and desires. In the first case, he reacts to stimuli in his environment and is determined by his experiences. This is the behavioral counselor's view of man—man reacting to outside forces and stimuli. Still viewed as a reactive being, man can be described quite differently as reacting to and controlled by his inner needs and drives, which are strongly influenced by previous experience with satisfaction or frustration. Psychoanalytic counselors hold this view of man. The second

---

[4]See C. H. Patterson, *Theories of Counseling and Psychotherapy* (New York: Harper & Row, Publishers, 1966) for the fullest up-to-date discussion of counseling theories.

[5]Patterson, *op. cit.*, pp. 488–89.

model Patterson describes as ". . . the image of man as a being-in-the-process-of-becoming—a view of man as personal, conscious, future-oriented."[6] Nondirective and existenial counselors look at man in this way.

With such different premises about the nature of man, counselors are bound to develop different approaches. Their predilection toward one model or the other may be based on explicit scientific, psychological, empirical, or religious grounds, or it may be implicit in their behavior. One's notions about the nature of man are personal and highly interrelated to one's values and beliefs. *Hence, one's counseling approach is also personal and, in order to be genuine, must be developed individually within the framework of one's own values and beliefs.* Whitehouse says it is the counselor ". . . who devises in accordance with his own interests, perceptions of the issues, and his own desires and needs."[7] Many beginning counselors make the mistake of trying to adopt a counseling approach which is alien to their approach to life.

Some counselors see counseling as essentially a rational process. If the counselee has the proper information thoughtfully interpreted to him, he will be able to make a rational decision based on this information. If the counselee is helped to understand why he behaves as he does, he will be able to change his behavior. Others see the counseling process as essentially affective, or concerned with emotion. As the counselee comes to understand and accept his feelings about himself and others, he is free to grow toward what he can be. In their thinking about the amount of rationality in the counseling process, counselors stand at all points between the two extremes of all reason and all feeling. No effective counselor can completely ignore either reason or feeling.

Some counselors believe that the counselee should be given full responsibility for the course of the counseling sessions. The counselee does the leading, knowing what he wants to talk about and when he is ready to bring up difficult or painful topics. He does his own interpreting. Others believe that a counselee who has come to the counselor because he needs help cannot be expected to assume the lead. They allow the counselee to assume more leadership as he demonstrates his ability to do so. Again,

[6]Patterson, *op. cit.*, p. 489.
[7]Frederick A. Whitehouse, "The Concept of Therapy: A Review of Some Essentials," *Rehabilitation Literature*, Vol. 28, No. 8 (August, 1967), 239.

counselors stand at all points between the extremes of complete counselee responsibility and complete counselor responsibility. But no effective counselor assumes complete control of his counselee nor allows him complete license.

In Chapter 1, we referred to the counselor as initiator of change. In their counseling role, counselors disagree as to the extent to which they should be involved in producing change. Some feel that *as counselors* their activities are confined to the counseling office in helping counselees understand and cope with the situation in which they live. Others believe that part of their role *as counselors* is to bring about change in the environment of the counselee that will change his behavior. A counselor may make suggestions to a teacher for treating an individual student differently, persuade the track coach to invite a boy out for the team, or try to effect changes in educational practices which he sees as harmful to his counselees.

Areas of Agreement   Although counselors differ in the amount of responsibility given to counselees, we can say that all counselors not only allow but expect counselees to make their own decisions. Even though decisions may be at variance with the counselor's best opinions and even his values, he believes in the counselee's right to decide for himself. He may help the counselee explore alternatives and consider the consequences of various choices. He may tell the counselee what he as a professional counselor believes to be the best course. He may concentrate on listening and trying to understand the counselee's world. But in the end, the counselor accepts the counselee's decision, except, of course, in cases where harm to himself or another person is involved.

There is a clear trend now in several counseling approaches toward assigning more responsibility to the counselee not only for what he becomes but for what he is now. Glasser has instituted a new approach which he calls *reality therapy* based on the idea that people who are in trouble can and must learn responsible behavior regardless of how traumatic their background may have been.[8] Krumboltz writes, "We shall expect students to feel an increased sense of responsibility for their

[8]William Glasser, *Reality Therapy, A New Approach to Psychiatry* (New York: Harper & Row, Publishers, 1965).

own actions."[9] Mowrer devotes a chapter to the rediscovery of responsiblity.[10]

Counselors vary, too, in the amount of control they think people have over their own lives. However, they agree that people can change—why else would they counsel? They are united in their conviction that change is possible for people though divided on how it takes place, or to what extent.

Closely allied to the conviction that people can change is agreement that counseling is a learning process. Counselors want counselees to learn enough during counseling to be better equipped to work out future problems more independently. They want counselees to become increasingly independent and self-directing. They do not, therefore, encourage dependence in counseling. They do not give advice or turn their skills into subtle persuasion toward counselor-determined directions.

A study by Fiedler suggests that the quality of the therapeutic relationship has more to do with expertness of psychotherapy than the approach used.[11] Experienced psychotherapists of different persuasions agreed that the relationship is basic to success. In looking, then, for areas of agreement, the importance of the counseling relationship to successful counseling stands out. Its importance overrides that of particular approaches or techniques. Recent studies confirm this importance and are beginning to identify the characteristics of successful counseling relationships.[12]

Some Different Approaches   *Directive counseling* approaches assume that the counselor is the professional who can help the counselee and is thus the one who gives direction to the interview. He brings to the encounter tests and other information which can aid in reaching decisions. After diagnosis of the problem, he offers his best opinion of possibilities open, alternatives, and consequences. It is an essentially rational approach.

Nondirective counseling approaches assume that the counselee

[9]John D. Krumboltz, ed., *Revolution in Counseling: Implications of Behavioral Science* (Boston: Houghton Mifflin Company, 1966) p. 9.

[10]O. Hobart Mowrer, *The New Group Therapy* (Princeton, N.J.: D. Van Nostrand Co., Inc., 1964).

[11]Fred E. Fiedler, "A Comparison of Therapeutic Relationships in Psychoanalytic, Nondirective, and Adlerian Therapy," *Journal of Consulting Psychology*, Vol. 14; No. 6 (December, 1950), 436–45.

[12]Robert R. Carkhuff and Bernard G. Berenson, *Beyond Counseling and Therapy* (New York: Holt, Rinehart & Winston, Inc., 1967).

has the capacity to work out his own problems given a situation where he feels free to do so. The counselor tries to create such a situation in the counseling processes. He focuses on counselees' feelings and attitudes and refrains from interjecting his opinion, using tests and other information only as counselees ask for it, and encouraging the counselee to give the direction he wants to the interviews.

Existentialist approaches assume that man is able to be responsible for his own behavior and future. These approaches are based more on an approach to life, an attitude, than on particular techniques. What is real is that man exists and has a choice about how he exists. Counselors from several different schools of counseling have been drawn by the possible contribution of existentialism, which itself covers a broad range of religious and philosophic thought.

Behavioral and *learning theory* approaches assume that man is a biological being who reacts to stimuli in his environment and whose behavior is conditioned by his experiences. What is known about learning is applied to counseling, which is viewed as a learning situation. The counselor helps counselees reach their goals through the use of positive re-enforcement, conditioning, desensitization, and models. Goals for counseling are mutually agreed upon by counselor and counselee and defined in terms of behavior change.

Eclectic approaches assume that counselors should use the approach best suited to help particular counselees with particular problems. They draw carefully from many approaches and adapt their counseling as necessary to the problem and the counselee.

Computer counseling, or the use of computers in direct interaction with students in the decision making process, is not an approach but needs to be recognized as a development that will be part of many schools within the next few years. Computers will not take the place of human counselors but may, if used thoughtfully, enable counselors to be more effective and relieve them of routine counseling. Loughary writes that the problem is to develop this new resource so as to ". . . assure that automated systems contribute to, rather than inhibit, the freedom of the individual."[13]

[13]John W. Loughary, Deloss Friesen, and Robert Hurst, "Autocoun: A Computer-Based Automated Counseling Simulation System," *Personnel and Guidance Journal*, Vol. 45, No. 1 (September, 1966), 15.

The Relationship is What Counts

What It Is   As we have read about counseling, listened to others counsel, and have ourselves counseled, various qualities have come to stand out as essential to the counseling relationship. Most of these are common to all good human relations but unfortunately do not occur as often as we might wish. These qualities are described in terms such as *sensitivity, caring, concern, love, compassion, nonjudgment, respect,* and *dignity.* They stem, again, from one's belief's about the nature of man. Whatever his beliefs are, it is essential that they lead the counselor to respect for the individual, concern for his fellow man, and genuine liking for people.

How do these attitudes communicate to the counselee? No matter how much the counselor loves his fellow man, if he does not somehow communicate this feeling to the counselee, his love is wasted—at least in the counseling relationship. Does he, then, verbalize his feelings? Tell his counselees that he has respect for all individuals? Assure them of his concern for them? Perhaps. He can indeed communicate some of his attitudes by his words, but he will communicate more surely through his actions. Somehow he has to prove he cares through the way in which he behaves during the counseling sessions.

How does he show his concern? One way a counselor shows his concern is to try to understand how things look to the counselee. To have someone really try to understand how you feel suggests that he really cares about you, enough to try to understand your world. Whether he succeeds or not is not as important as whether or not he tries. Haven't you felt a lift when someone said something like, "Yeah, I see what you mean. It really seems as if everything were working against you." Instead of giving you easy reassurance that everything will get better soon, he understands how discouraged you are. He cares enough to share your discouragement, and with this sharing and understanding, you feel more able to face whatever troubles are besetting you. Whether or not you are justified in feeling discouraged is beside the point. This other person accepts the way you feel now, the way things look to you. He does not analyze, he does not pry. He tries to understand.

To try to understand means listening. Who do you know who will listen intently to what you have to say for an hour without interposing his own thoughts? A counselor listens for what the counselee is saying with his words, actions, and facial expressions. He listens for what is behind the words. Really listening to what a person is saying is one way of demonstrating respect and concern. The counselor is showing that he believes the counselee has something important to say, that he has something to contribute to the course of the counseling sessions. Listening is not easy; on the contrary, it is hard work. It is one of the hardest things a counselor has to learn.

Teachers find it particularly difficult because their usual relationship with students does not involve listening in the same way that counseling does. They are more used to telling than to listening, and when listening, listening for right answers rather than what students are trying to tell them. Our society in general encourages more talking than listening. If you observe for the next few days, we predict that you will find few people who *really* listen to you and that you will discover that you yourself do little listening.

A counselor demonstrates respect by treating what a counselee says with respect. He tries to understand. *He listens.* Because his focus is on trying to understand, he is not concerned with making judgements about the worth of the counselee. He accepts him for what he is though he may not agree with some of his actions or beliefs. He is interested in him as a person. Whether or not the counselor voices his disagreement is not important as long as his basic concern for the person of the counselee is clear. The counselor who says, "Really, a person with an attitude like yours is hardly worth my time," is unlikely to develop a counseling relationship with that person. The psychiatrist who reports that an adolescent was too impudent for him to work with is unlikely to create confidence in the adolescent.

A counselor who treats what is said to him confidentially is also showing respect for the counselee. He respects him enough to take what he says seriously and not relay it to other people. Much of the counseling relationship is based on mutual confidence and trust. Each must feel that he can speak freely. Surely, a counselee is not going to discuss those things closest and most important to him unless he is sure that the counselor will not repeat what he has heard. An adolescent may not want his parents to know that he is worried about their quarrels. A wife may not want her husband to know that she is even talking with a counselor. A counselor hears many things which he must keep to himself or else betray a confidence. Confidentiality is an essential of the counseling relationship.

Rogers identifies four characteristics of counseling relationships where counseling had been judged successful—*congruence, empathy, positive regard,* and *unconditionality of regard.*[14] *Congruence* is being yourself in the counseling situation, being honest and sincere. Your real self and that which you show the counselee are as congruent, as close together, as possible. In letting the counselee see you as you are, he is more free to show himself as he is. It involves self-revelation and openness on the part of the counselor. *Empathy* is seeing the world as the other person sees it, putting yourself in his shoes, not sympathizing, but understanding how things look to him. *Positive regard* means looking at the counselee in a generally positive way, caring for him and believing in him. *Unconditionality of regard* means that no strings are put on your regard for the other person. You do not say that you will like him only if he does certain things of which you approve.

Positive regard and unconditionality of regard together are similar to one of the Greek words for love, *agape.* Love in this sense does not mean love as it is often used today. It is neither sentimental nor erotic. It is love, concern, and regard for another person without thought of reward or return from that person. It does not even mean that you necessarily like the other person. You do respect him.

What It Is Not   The counseling relationship is not anarchic. As described above, it allows for a wide range of control, but there must be some control in the counseling situation. All our talk of love, empathy, and compassion does not mean that counselors let counselees do anything they want to do. A psychiatrist once described his early supervised experiences in counseling a particular child. He came out each day with his tie awry, clothes mussed and sandy, his hair on end. His supervisor asked him what in the world happened. He replied that the child was angry and expressing his hostility, to which the supervisor replied, "Being permissive doesn't mean letting him tear you apart. Control him next time even if you have to sit on him."

Some counselors are very permissive, allowing a wide range of activity and verbalization. They may allow a child to hit the

[14]Carl R. Rogers, "The Interpersonal Relationship: The Core of Guidance," *Harvard Educational Review,* Vol. 32, No. 4 (Fall, 1962), 416–29.

table with a hammer, but will not allow themselves to be hit with the hammer. They may allow an adolescent to curse but not allow him to disturb others in nearby rooms. Other counselors set clear limits immediately: "You may say whatever you feel, but I cannot allow you to curse." Setting limits within which you are comfortable is being congruent. Whatever limits are set, concern and caring can still be present.

Good counseling ought not to create a dependency relationship where either party has a continuing need for the other. The relationship is one without strings. The counselor is free to see the counselee assume independence and go on his way. The counselee finds that he is free to direct his life in the best way for him. Within the counseling relationship, he becomes more able to work out his own problems and concerns independent of a counselor.

The Helping Relationship   In his book *On Becoming a Person*, Rogers associates the counseling relationship with every kind of helping relationship, that is, ". . . a relationship in which at least one of the parties has the intent of promoting the growth, development, maturity, improved functioning, improved coping with life of the other.[15] People involved in this kind of relationship are doctors, psychotherapists, ministers, and parents. He includes teachers though he wonders if all teachers are interested in promoting growth.

We assume that you who are reading this book and who either **are** or will soon become teachers will be primarily concerned with promoting growth of your students. An understanding of the characteristics of the counseling or helping relationship can help you work toward a relationship in your classroom which is growth-promoting. The kind of environment thus engendered is obviously a favorable one for learning.

In a School Setting

Sam was a good enough student to be placed in advanced classes when he started junior high school. At the end of his first marking period, his grades were good. Thereafter, his grades gradually declined and he did his homework carelessly if at all. Mrs. Minella, his English teacher, was particularly concerned about

[15]Carl R. Rogers, *On Becoming a Person* (Boston: Houghton Mifflin Company, 1961) pp. 39–40.

his drop in performance since she had earlier been impressed by the quality and imagination of his work. She called him in after school to tell him that if he did not improve she would have to recommend that he be dropped from the advanced class. Other teachers told him the same thing. When his work continued to decline, Mrs. Minella referred him to his school counselor, Mr. Warshower.

Counseling in a school setting involves some dimensions and problems that are less prominent in a child guidance or mental health clinic. If we follow through on the case of Sam, we can learn about these different dimensions and problems.

Differing Expectations   In any counseling situation, the participants approach it with varying expectations. Each one may have different hopes. The counselor looks for greater self-understanding on the part of the counselee. The counselee looks for sympathy and help. The parents look for improved behavior on the part of their child. The nonschool counselor understands these different expectations but is essentially concerned only with those of his counselee and himself.

The school counselor also works with different expectations but there is one big difference. He is in daily contact not only with his counselees but with his counselee's peers, teachers, and often his parents. He is involved with them in the same school situation. Each person knows that the others have contacts or relationships with those who know him.

In addition, each person has different pressures on him. Let's look at each of the people in the case of Sam. Since we don't really know them, we can only guess and use our guesses to understand better what stake each person has in Sam's interviews with Mr. Warshower and how this may affect Mr. Warshower's behavior. From understanding this case, we can generalize about the special problems of counseling in an educational setting.

Mrs. Minella, as a teacher, wants Sam to do the work of which he is capable. Moreover, she is under pressure from the administration to produce good academic achievement on the part of her students. Understanding though she may be, Sam's declining grades can constitute a threat to her. Will her departmental chairman think she is not doing her job? Why doesn't Sam respond to her? Is there something the matter with her teaching? When she refers Sam to his counselor, she is likely to hope that counseling will disclose what is wrong, improve his work, and free her of any possible blame.

Sam's declining grades suggest that something is wrong in his world. We have no way thus far of knowing what it might be. As a student, he is always under pressure to achieve. Why is he responding in this way? What does he hope for in counseling? To begin with, he did not ask for counseling. He has been referred to his counselor. Instead of having any hopes, he may resent this referral. Who are these people butting into his life? That's all adults do. Why can't they leave him alone? On the other hand, he may have hoped deep down inside that someone would help him. He may have been asking for help in the only way he knew how which was by doing poor work. What he may look for in counseling, then, depends on his feelings about his referral and also on what he knows about his counselor. Is he a good guy? Is he someone Sam feels he can talk with? Does he know him?

Sam's friends may influence some of Sam's expectations of counseling. He will have heard from some of them about Mr. Warshower. If they trust him, Sam will be more likely to trust him. Some of them may have been counseled. How will Sam's friends feel about his seeing Mr. Warshower? Will they accept it? Will they deride him?

Sam's parents want the best for their child. They may be under pressure to have Sam do well. They hope for so much for him. They may worry about his grades or they may not care at all. They would like to be able to help him. What can the school counselor offer? They hope that he will get Sam back to work.

Mr. Warshower schedules an appointment with Sam. When Sam taps on Mr. Warshower's door, all this comes tapping with him: pressures for achievement on the part of Sam, possibly his parents, and his teachers; possible resentment on the part of all; hopes for improved performance; and, for Sam, whatever problems and concerns are besetting him. If Mr. Warshower is a good counselor, he knows all this but focuses on Sam himself. He wants to listen to Sam and to understand with him how he sees school and life. He wants to help Sam work out his concerns in whatever way is best for him even if this way does not include improved performance.

In this way, he is no different from his colleague in the mental health clinic but he is not screened as the clinic counselor is from the significant others in Sam's life. He will see them often, work with them on other projects, and mix with them informally in the teachers' lounge, the hall, the cafeteria, and the school dances. If his expectations are radically different from those of the other adults concerned with Sam, he has to somehow work out these differences. If a nonschool counselor antagonizes a teacher, it matters little. If a school counselor antagonizes a teacher, he may lose some of his effectiveness as a school counselor, not so much in his counseling role as in his consulting and coordinating role. He does more than counsel and has to remember that the significant others in Sam's life are also the people with whom he works daily in many different kinds of ways. Moreover, if he loses the trust or respect of very many teachers he is likely to lose much of his clientele. Teachers will not regard him as a person they want to talk with themselves or to whom they would send students for help. Teacher distrust of counselors can also be communicated to students.

Some misunderstanding about expectations derives from what appear to be, and sometimes are, differing values. A teacher may hold academic achievement as more important than a student's self-acceptance. Actually, both are important in a student's development as a person. A teacher may see a counselor as a person who does not hold students to accepted values because the counselor allows students to make decisions contrary to the teacher's values.

A teacher may feel that a student who, after counseling, decides to drop out of school in the eleventh grade should have been urged by his counselor to finish his high school education, an education which becomes more essential each year. Counselors and teachers may disagree on the extent to which they should attempt to influence students' decisions. In the end, however, a student must make his own decision. He cannot be forced to stay in school. In cases like this, discussion between the teacher and counselor can help each understand the other's approach and values.

Communication   All counselors are concerned with communication, but school counselors more so than others. They must, of course, communicate to their counselees that they accept them, are concerned about them, and care. They must be able to receive communication from their counselees and listen to what they are trying to say. Each must come to understand the other's expectations of counseling. This is part of developing a counseling relationship.

If Mr. Warshower allows Sam to decide, after careful consideration, to change to regular classes when Mrs. Minella expects him to urge Sam to stay in advanced classes and study, then a breakdown in communication between counselor and teacher is likely, a breakdown which will spread as Mrs. Minella tells in the teachers' lounge of Mr. Warshower's lack of support. This kind of breakdown can be avoided if teachers understand what the counselor is trying to do, if they understand his contribution to the school and he understands their contribution. Teachers need to understand what counseling is. When they do, they are less likely to expect of counseling what it cannot provide. Discussion between Mrs. Minella and Mr. Warshower before Mr. Warshower sees Sam can help clarify expectations on both sides.

Avenues of communication between the counselor and significant others must be open so that each is free to talk openly to the other. Keeping communication open is largely the responsibility of the counselor. One of his competencies is facilitating communication. Teachers too have some responsibility for open communication. If they have complaints about guidance and counseling services, they should talk with the counselor rather than gripe in the teachers' room. If they have questions about what the counselors are doing, they should ask their questions of the counselors. Communication is obviously a two-way street.

In the case of Sam, it is important that Mrs. Minnella discuss her concern about Sam honestly with Mr. Warshower, that Mr. Warshower discuss honestly his concern about Sam, that the parents feel free to talk with Mr. Warshower, and that Sam be helped to talk freely with Mr. Warshower, Mrs. Minella, and his parents.

This openness of communication is important in school counseling, but it occasions another difference between school and other counseling.

Confidentiality   School counselors in most states do not have privileged communication, that is, unlike doctors, priests, and lawyers, they may be required by law to divulge the content of counseling sessions. Nonetheless, confidentiality is absolutely essential to the counseling relationship. If Sam is to feel that he can talk about his concerns, he must believe that what he says in Mr. Warshower's office will go no further without his consent.

Problems of confidentiality are not fully settled in the literature on counseling and are settled in practice only by the best judgment of the people involved. Mr. Warshower learns from Sam that he so resents the pressure and heavy load of assignments in the advanced classes that he has given up studying. He wants to read other things besides the books assigned in class. He has no time for his own pursuits. He does not think learning should be as competitive as it appears to him to be among the advanced students so he refuses to play the game. Mr. Warshower can help Sam work through his thinking about school and his reaction to it. He can discuss with him alternatives to his present response. Sam may decide to go along with things or to change some of his classes.

What bothers Mr. Warshower now is that Sam is disclosing feelings that Mrs. Minella might like to know about. She may not realize how students react to the demands of advanced work. As a good teacher, she wants her students to enjoy learning, not resent it. Hearing Sam's point of view might change her approach in these classes, thereby benefiting herself and her other students. But Mr. Warshower has promised Sam confidentiality.

Mr. Warshower can do one of several things, depending on his best judgment. He can maintain confidentiality without question. He can ask Sam if it is all right with him if he discusses what Sam has said with Mrs. Minella. He can ask Sam to talk with Mrs. Minella himself or arrange a three-way conference. A final alternative is to talk with Mrs. Minella as the professional colleague that she should be. As the teacher who referred Sam, she is entitled to some feedback and help in knowing how to deal with Sam if he remains in her classroom. Mr. Warshower should be able to trust a teacher's discretion and understanding. From other experience, he probably knows that he can trust some and not others. What he does, then, depends on what he knows of the situation and the people.

Teachers who understand counseling will understand the crucial role of confidentiality in the counseling process. Whatever counselors share with them as professional colleagues, they will regard as confidential. Confidentiality is equally essential in the use of test scores and other information which may be helpful to teachers in working with their students. Where teachers have misused confidence placed in them by talking about students in the teachers' lounge or by repeating to students what the counselor has said in confidence, counselors learn not to trust teachers and students learn not to trust counselors or teachers. Thus, a continually wider wall of mistrust is built which hampers the effectiveness of both teacher and counselor.

School counselors are constantly confronted with problems of confidentiality. The problem becomes larger and trickier, however, where transgressions of school regulations or actual crimes are concerned. Suppose a student tells a counselor that the seniors are planning to boycott classes the next day? Or that he knows who is selling drugs in the parking lot? Or that she is pregnant? Or that her friend is pregnant? Or that he has been stealing cars? In cases like these, which are far from unusual, the school counselor may feel torn by conflicting loyalties.

The school counselor works within the school community and is supervised, hired, and paid by school officials. Is not his responsibility when he hears from a counselee of some impending damage to the school to alert school officials? But if he does so, the student knows he has broken his promise of confidentiality and his reputation as a trusted counselor is tarnished. Our response to this predicament is that the school hired him to be a counselor and ought to know that confidentiality is essential to his success and usefulness as a counselor. He ought not to be expected to betray an individual counselee's confidence *unless there is a clear danger to the counselee or to someone else*. He must, then, judge when there is this kind of danger. He is loyal to the school if he does the best job of counseling he knows how to do. If school staff members do not understand the need for confidentiality in counseling, then the counselor must endeavor to convey this understanding to them.

When school counselors get a general picture from their counselees of poor or dangerous situations in the school, then it is indeed their responsibility to tell the responsible people about this situation and to help to bring about change. They need not betray individual confidences in so doing.

Discipline   In order for learning to take place, order, that is, discipline, must be maintained in a school. Maintenance of order involves rules and enforcement. Teachers, administrators, secretaries, and custodians are all involved in discipline. School counselors have often insisted that they not be involved in discipline because they feel that disciplining will detract from the counseling relationships they try to build with students. How can a student confide in the person who may also discipline him?

Will students who see the counselor maintaining order in the cafeteria or the halls see him as a person with whom they wish to share their concerns? On the other hand, how will teachers feel about school counselors who dissociate themselves from unpleasant chores such as hall or cafeteria duty?

The problem we have here is how the school counselor relates himself to the disciplinary concerns of the school situation within which he works. The way in which he does this depends in part on the kind of discipline maintained and the way in which it is enforced. If the rules are unreasonable and harshly enforced, he may want to dissociate himself from enforcing them and, at the same time, work to bring about change. Interested as he is in a favorable climate for learning, he knows that harsh discipline interferes with rather than promotes learning. He knows that order is necessary but knows too that the best order comes with understanding and agreement of those involved: students, teachers, parents. Moreover, he talks with many students whose only problems are those produced by the school. In this case, the school counselor can do more for students by trying to change the situation than by only listening to them.

If the discipline of the school is reasonable, the school counselor may play several roles. He may interpret school policies to parents and students. He may counsel with students who are discipline problems on the assumption that their behavior is a cry for help. (The worse an adolescent behaves, the louder he may be asking for help). He may consult with teachers, helping them to know how to work with disruptive students in the classroom.

Nearly everyone agrees that school counselors ought not to administer punishment, that is, have responsibility for expulsion, suspension, detention after school, or other punishments. It is highly appropriate, however, for the school counselor to give background information on students to the person responsible for discipline so that he can make informed judgments. The counselor may often have information which would make suspension, for example, unwise. Beyond this point, the amount of involvement in discipline is debatable. We think school counselors ought to be as responsible as any other adult in the school for reacting to disorder in the halls such as a boy pushing a girl into a locker or a fight starting. But should he report a boy he finds smoking in the washroom?

Each counselor and school has to work out the counselor's relation to discipline. Different situations will require different answers. Whatever the situation, the counselor should not be seen as the "bad guy," the one who hands out punishment, for surely this would limit his ability to form good counseling relationships. And he ought to remember always that his first responsibility is to the individual student.

Teacher Complaints   School counselors are expected to listen to students who come to them or who are sent to them. They listen without criticizing the student or cutting him off from what he would like to say. Therefore, they hear complaints about teachers.

> She hates my guts.
> She doesn't know what she's talking about.
> He says you can disagree with him, but boy, does he get mad if you do.
> You can't even move your chair in that class.
> All the kids hate him.
> She told me I was stupid.

And so on. In listening and trying to understand how the classroom looks to the student, the counselor is doing his job of counseling. Teachers who understand this and who in addition trust the counselor will not be unduly concerned. They know that listening does not necessarily mean agreeing. They trust the counselor not to tell the principal of every little complaint. They appreciate feedback from the counselor that may help them be better teachers. Teachers who do not understand counseling may, understandably enough, feel threatened and accuse the counselor of being a crying towel. It looks to them as if every time a student gets mad at a teacher, he runs to the counselor.

Interestingly enough, the student who finds a ready listener in his counselor is often able to gain a better perspective on the situation.

> She's not so bad once you get the hang of her.
> I guess we do make it sort of hard on him.
> I can't blame him for getting mad sometimes.

Occasionally, counselors will hear many serious complaints from many students about one teacher. There is little agreement about the counselor's responsibility in this case. We believe that if there is any possibility that a teacher is actually damaging students by his treatment of them, the school counselor is obligated to bring the situation to the attention of a responsible person such as the departmental chairman or the principal. Just whom he sees and how he goes about it depend upon his knowledge of the people involved, and his skill in working with them.

Forced Referrals   Believing that it is difficult to help people unless they want to be helped, counselors prefer to work with those who have referred themselves, that is, who have voluntarily come to a counselor for help. Many high school students, however, are referred to their counselors by teachers or administrators. If a student feels that he has been sent to a counselor because he has been bad, he is not likely to be in a mood to be helped regardless of how much he could use help. He sees the counselor as one more adult lined up against him. It takes special skill on the counselor's part to communicate his genuine desire to help and his willingness to listen to the student's side. If he is able to do this, the counseling may proceed as if the student has referred himself. In effect, this is the case if the counselor gives him the choice of continuing or dropping the counseling once the possibilities have been explained. A study by Arbuckle showed significant improvements in behavior on the part of students referred for counseling as major behavior problems, which supports the idea that nonvoluntary counseling can be effective.[16]

How much of a handicap forced referrals are depends a great deal on how they are handled by the teacher. A thoughtful referral is the best start for successful counseling. A teacher who brings a student to the guidance office with the remark, "Maybe *you* can help him!" makes it awkward for both counselor and student. An introduction such as, "I wonder if you can help Bill work out some of the problems he and I are having in class," sets a better tone for beginning a counseling relationship.

Educational-Vocational Planning   Although all kinds of problems come within school counselors' ken, a preponderance of their counseling centers around educational and vocational decisionmaking. They are particularly concerned, then, with the

---

[16]Dugald S. Arbuckle and Angelo V. Boy, "Client-Centered Therapy in Counseling Students with Behavior Problems," *Journal of Counseling Psychology*, Vol. 8, No. 2 (Summer, 1961), 136–39.

process of decisionmaking and in teaching their counselees how to make decisions. That high school students receive help in decisionmaking is clearly essential to their future welfare. High school years are filled with crucial decisions which determine in part the course of their lives. Some decisions are well-nigh irreversible. The student who is sure that he does not want to go to college and takes general or nonacademic courses makes college entrance difficult if he later changes his mind.

School counselors need to be particularly well informed on school curriculum, college requirements and characteristics, and occupational trends and opportunities. They are expected to be able to direct students to the proper sources of information and to have many of these sources at hand in the guidance office. They should also be able to call on teachers for information in their particular field about career opportunities and training.

In Groups

Working with small groups of counselees rather than with one counselee at a time is of increasing interest to school counselors. Although a few schools have experimented with group counseling for a number of years, group counseling has not been widespread. Interest is growing rapidly now, with more reports of successful group counseling and more research on what it is and how it proceeds. Group therapy is increasingly used in coordination with individual counseling in mental hospitals, agencies and clinics.

Group counseling has been defined by Gazda, Duncan, and Meadows in a composite statement derived from a survey designed to gain information about the present status of group counseling:

> Group counseling is a dynamic, interpersonal process focusing on conscious thought and behavior and involving the therapy functions of permissiveness, orientation to reality, catharsis, and mutual trust, caring, understanding, acceptance, and support. The therapy functions are created and nurtured in a small group through the sharing of personal concerns with one's peers and the counselor(s). The group counselees are basically normal individuals with various concerns which are not debilitating to the extent of requiring extensive personality change. The group counselees may ultilize the group interaction

to increase understanding and acceptance of values and goals and to learn and/or unlearn certain attitudes and behaviors.[17]

Most of what we have said thus far about counseling holds true for group counseling. It is an encounter, but with more than two people involved. The varying approaches to counseling described earlier apply to group counseling. The quality of the relationship remains crucial to successful outcomes.

Just as it is useful for teachers to understand what takes place in individual counseling, so it is also useful for them to understand the nature of group counseling. As school counselors work more frequently with small groups, teachers will hear more about group counseling. If Mrs. Howe refers Susan to her counselor, Susan might be placed in group counseling with students who have similar problems. Some high schools are experimenting with sensitivity training groups, human relations workshops, and black-white encounter groups. (These kinds of groups are discussed in the final chapter.) These groups, though closely allied to group counseling, are not identical in either goals or methods; however, many of the same skills and understandings are relevant. With the increase in small groups, teachers may be called upon to participate in some way. If so, they should understand something about group counseling. In addition, in-service training with a school counselor or psychologist would be highly desirable.

In many schools, counselors or teachers meet with groups of students to discuss vocational decisions, school regulations, test results, college admissions requirements, dating practices, parental relations, etc. This kind of activity is usually called *group guidance*, occuring sometimes in regular classrooms, sometimes in homerooms, sometimes in guidance classes. It is an important part of guidance and counseling services in providing information to students and a forum for discussion of common problems. Group guidance needs to be distinguished, however, from group counseling. The focus, rather than on sharing personal concerns with one's peers and counselor, is on content and relatively general and impersonal concerns. Dating in general may be discussed but not one's feelings about a particular date. College

[17]George M. Gazda, Jack A. Duncan, and M. Eugene Meadows, "Group Counseling and Group Procedures—Report of a Survey," *Counselor Education and Supervision*, Vol. 6, No. 4 (Summer, 1967), 306.

choice in general may be discussed but not usually one's own concerns about success in college. The differences are well discussed by Goldman who points out that, in work in groups, content is on a continuum from usual school subjects to school-related topics such as college choice, to nonschool topics such as dating.[18] Process is on a continuum from leader-dominated discussion to leader and group cooperation, to origination of topics from the group members. Group guidance is toward the middle whereas group counseling is toward the end. In group counseling, the topics are likely to be nonschool topics originating from the group.

Not all counselors are successful in working with groups. Some are more comfortable in a one-to-one relationship. Group counselors have a difficult task in listening carefully to each participant, ensuring that each has a chance to speak and is listened to by others, and setting the tone of mutual respect and concern which is necessary to group counseling. Not all counselees react favorably to group counseling. Counselors have to be thoughtful in involving those in group counseling who are most likely to receive benefit. One study suggests that less dogmatic people, that is, those with open minds, are more able to participate in group counseling than those with closed minds.[19]

Until recently, we have been cautioned not to regard group counseling as a substitute for individual work. Mowrer, however, suggests that group counseling begin as soon as possible, perhaps after two or three individual sessions, so that the counselee is introduced into a growth-promoting group situation where he can test out his interactions with other people.[20] If much of a person's troubles and concerns are based on unsatisfactory interpersonal relationships, then it makes sense to let him join with a group of his peers under the leadership of a sensitive counselor. In the safety of this group he can find acceptance which he has often missed elsewhere and work out his interpersonal relationships in a more natural setting than when he is with just one person. He says things that he has not said elsewhere and finds the group interested and receptive. He learns

[18]Leo Goldman, "Group Guidance: Content and Process," *Personnel and Guidance Journal*, Vol. 40, No. 6 (February, 1962), 518–22.
[19]C. Gratton Kemp, "Behaviors in Group Guidance (Socio Process) and Group Counseling (Psyche Process)," *Journal of Counseling Psychology*, Vol. 10, No. 4 (Winter, 1963), 373–77.
[20]O. Hobart Mowrer, *The New Group Therapy*, (Princeton, N.J.: D. Van Nostrand Co., Inc., 1964) p. 162.

that others may have the same worries and concerns that he does, if not worse ones. Participants speak to each other in a blunt way:

> You'd be a fool to quit school, Joe.
> Why don't you ever give anyone else a chance?
> So we've all got problems.

Members accept comments like these from each other when they might not from an adult.

What makes a group become this kind of group, where people feel free to bring out their concerns and faults without being ridiculed or rejected? Groups like this are found not only in counseling but also in self-help groups such as Alcoholics Anonymous. In group counseling, the leader is instrumental in setting the tone. Group members test him to see if he is really sincere in saying they can talk freely, and finding him sincere go on to find growth in this freedom of expression. They learn to accept others' comments and feelings as they watch the leader accept comments and feelings. In self-help groups the eagerness to help others of those who have themselves been in the depths of despair is instrumental in providing an atmosphere of concern and acceptance. Stewart and Warnath point out that for a group to give its members more than they might learn individually, ". . . they must have a feeling of interdependence and be aware of some common purpose or goal."[21]

Group counseling needs more research. We do not know enough about optimal group size, whether or not group members should have same or different problems, how often or how long groups should meet, or what successful ways of initiating and forming groups are. Nonetheless, group counseling has proved successful in a number of school situations. School counselors and psychologists have initiated work with groups of underachievers, potential dropouts, behavior problems, and parents of behavior problems. A counselor of our acquaintance working with groups of underachievers found that three out of four participants improved their grades. Cohn describes extensive group counseling in Westchester County, New York.[22] At Mas-

[21]Lawrence H. Stewart and Charles F. Warnath, *The Counselor and Society: A Cultural Approach* (Boston: Houghton Mifflin Company, 1965) pp. 299–300.
[22]Benjamin Cohn and A. Mead Sniffen, "A School Report on Group Counseling," *Personnel and Guidance Journal*, Vol. XVI, No. 2, (October, 1962), 133–38.

sapequa High School in New York, 158 failing students were assigned to group counseling led by volunteers from the teachers and counselors who met with the school psychologist for training sessions. Many of these students improved their school work and wished to continue in group counseling. At Baldwin Junior High School in New York, counselors worked for a semester with two groups of potential dropouts. Three years later, the boys were still in school. In reviewing recent research, Kagan concludes that group procedures resulted in better client grade point averages, attitudes, knowledge, and behavior depending on the clients, the counselor, and the setting.[23]

Adolescents are particularly suited for group counseling because they are in the midst of working out their relationships with each other, the opposite sex, and their parents. Often painfully unsure of themselves in social situations, in the group they have a chance to practice and experience acceptance. Also, joined with others of their own age, they feel more equal with the school counselor who, no matter how understanding, is still an adult and associated with the power structure of the school. Culturally deprived youngsters often respond better to group counseling than to a one-to-one counseling situation. Kemp writes that ". . . experience in leadership training, changing food habits, work production, criminality, alcoholism, and prejudices all indicate that it is easier for some individuals to change when formed into a group than to change separately."[24]

Group counseling has potential for improving guidance and counseling services in the schools. It is unrealistic to expect all counseling to occur individually with present and foreseen counselor loads, and yet we will see the need for counseling among adolescents. Group counseling can expand the influence of the counselor. This process can achieve some goals that individual counseling cannot by providing a therapeutic group situation where interpersonal relationships can be strengthened. However, group counseling is not a panacea. It does not decrease counselor load, for group participants often come individually to the counselor as they come to know and trust him in the group situation. Time, thought, and skill are needed to organize and lead groups.

[23]Norman Kagan, "Group Procedures," *Review of Educational Research*, Vol. 36, No. 2 (April, 1966), 274–87.
[24]C. Gratton Kemp, *Intangibles in Counseling* (Boston: Houghton Mifflin Company, 1967), p. 156.

In comparing the relative effectiveness of individual and group counseling, Tyler concludes that one is about as effective as the other.[25] With this knowledge and with an increasingly impressive array of successful experiences with group counseling, school counselors will want to move toward improving their skills and expanding their services in and through group counseling.

SUMMARY

Counseling is an encounter in which the counselor helps the counselee begin to work out the problems or concerns which he brings to the counselor. The goal is to help the counselee arrive at solutions, answers, plans, decisions, or understandings which are satisfactory *to him.* Counselors respond in varying ways to their counselees depending on their counseling approach, which in turn depends on their view of the nature and behavior of man. Each counselor adopts or develops an approach which suits him.

Whatever the approach, successful counseling demands a good relationship between counselor and counselee. The counseling relationship is described in terms such as *sensitivity, caring, concern, love, compassion, respect,* and *dignity.* It is essential to the relationship that counselors demonstrate sincerity, openness, and understanding for the other person.

Counseling in a school setting presents problems not so commonly found in clinic or mental health center settings. The counselor in a school, rather than being associated only with the counselee, must work closely with the significant others in his counselee's lives. This frequently causes problems centering around communication between the counselor and significant others concerning expectations of counseling, confidentiality, discipline, and teacher complaints.

Group counseling has potential for improving guidance and counseling services in the schools. It has proved successful in a number of school districts. Many counselees find change easier in a group situation than in a one-to-one relationship.

An understanding of the counseling process, both individual and group, can help teachers work more effectively with the adolescents whom they teach.

[25]Leona Tyler, *The Work of the Counselor,* 3rd ed. (New York: Appleton-Century-Crofts, 1969), p. 234.

SUGGESTED READINGS

Arbuckle, Dugald S., *Counseling: Philosophy, Theory and Practice*. Boston: Allyn & Bacon, Inc., 1965.
A thorough, scholarly discussion of counseling with much to contribute to both skilled and novice counselors. More attention to philosophy and theoretical issues than most texts. Frequent examples of counseling.

Brammer, Lawrence A., and Everett L. Shostrom, *Therapeutic Psychology*. Englewood Cliffs, N.J.: Prentice-Hall, Inc., 1968.
An excellent presentation of individual and group counseling as helping people with a broad range of philosophical concerns as they move toward self-actualization.

Carkhoff, Robert R., and Bernard G. Berenson, *Beyond Counseling and Therapy*. New York: Holt, Rinehart & Winston, Inc., 1967.
Discusses characteristics of interpersonal effectiveness. Unusually helpful examination of strengths and weaknesses of different counseling approaches.

Glasser, William, *Reality Therapy*. New York: Harper & Row, Publishers, 1965.
A new approach which does not accept the concept of mental illness and focuses on the development of responsibility.

Kemp, C. Gratton, *Intangibles in Counseling*. Boston: Houghton Mifflin Company, 1967.
A discussion of such things as concepts of man, will, conscience, love, freedom and responsibility, as they relate to counseling concerns. The kind of book from which one can gain personal insight.

Krumboltz, John D., ed., *Revolution in Counseling*. Boston: Houghton Mifflin Company, 1966.
A series of papers presented at Stanford University describing and reacting to innovations in counseling, particularly behavioral counseling.

3

The Needs of Adolescents

From an adult's point of view, it is easy to make a case for adolescents' needing counseling. One dips into literature, popular or professional; one talks with those who are associated with adolescents; one is simply around adolescents for a time as are teachers. Knowledge gained from the above sources is then compiled. The result appears to be that "something should be done" about the difficulties and problems associated with this stage of growing up. Adults who are really interested in adolescents generally assume a helping rather than a punitive stance. This, combined with the reputation which counseling has acquired as being a helpful procedure, almost automatically brings to mind the idea that adolescents need to participate in such a process where they can work out their problems and concerns.

Whether the adolescent sees himself as being in need of such help is another matter. Just like other groups, there are some members who suffer so much misery that they grab at any panacea—even that of entering into a counseling relationship with an adult. A great majority of young people, however, would rather put up with their discomfort, relieve themselves by means of aggressive or withdrawal reactions, or depend upon their peers for counsel and understanding. If they do see counseling by adults as having a place in their lives, it is in connection with educational and occupational needs rather than with personal development.[1]

The need for educational-occupational counseling should not be minimized, and perhaps the relationship between such a need and personal growth should be recognized more than the average adolescent tends to. Somehow a dichotomy has arisen between types of counseling in the minds of both those to be counseled and those who counsel. Counseling can be partitioned no more than the counselee. So actually a person who sees himself in need of any type of counseling presents himself wholly to the counselor for assistance. It may, however, be less threatening to present one's need as that of planning for an educational or vocational future than to verbalize a need for personal growth. Adults must be sensitive to the fact that an adolescent who expresses need for the former may in actuality be asking for an opportunity to discuss other aspects of his development.

Teachers and, unfortunately, many school counselors often perceive personal-growth counseling as dealing with educational-vocational decisions or with the bizarre or deviant student.[2] It is not surprising that the same attitude prevails among adolescents. For many, consultation with a counselor about schedules, college choice, and job decisions is a fairly respectable procedure. Consultation with a counselor about personal or family problems is scorned and the idea that talking things over with such an adult might make development easier and more beneficial is simply not thought of. After all, who's such a "kook" as to need counseling about these kind of things? And even when the adolescent would welcome assistance with some of the things that bother him, how can he expect adults who have made such messes of their own lives to help him do any better?

Professional counselors are trained to anticipate these common kinds of attitudes. They learn to regard criticism toward adults as a normal phenomenon highly related to the adolescent's preoccupation with peer group values. Counselors are prepared

[1]Claude W. Grant, "How Students Perceive the Counselor's Role," *Personnel and Guidance Journal*, Vol. 33 (1954), 386–88.

[2]F. P. Robinson, "Guidance For All In Principle and In Practice," *Personnel and Guidance Journal*, Vol. 31 (1953), 500–504.

to "listen out" negative expressions until the adolescent can make a more positive approach to what is really troubling him.

Common Adult Viewpoints Toward Adolescents

At this point, it might be wise to take a look at the adults with whom the adolescent might have a chance to communicate. Leaving out the professional counselor, a listing of the others who might counsel consists of parents, lay youth leaders, and professionals whose primary business is not counseling, such as doctors, ministers, directors of personnel and youth organizations, and teachers. Any person holding such a position is likely to be approached by an adolescent who is in need of help. It therefore behooves this person to become sensitized as to the kind of adolescent he is dealing with. Understanding of, and knowledge about, persons to be counseled are essential if any counseling is to take place. How do these and other members of the adult society look upon adolescents? How do adult concepts of the adolescent compare with the way he really is?

Adults have differing views of adolescents. Sometimes they look upon the youth-adult relationship as being a kind of contest in which the adult must keep at least one jump ahead of the young person as he argues, cajoles, and appeals for privilege. What adult has not wished for a quicker brain when confronted with the lack of logic between expressed standards and actual practices, or the age-old cry of "everybody's doing it"? Sometimes the adolescent years are considered as a period of conflict which must be endured with resignation and hopefulness that major points of difficulty will be outgrown. How often we hear something like: "All 15-year-olds are like that. Just give him another year and he'll be all right."

Many adults feel keenly that the adolescent totally rejects them, that he enjoys their errors and makes fun of their behavior. They pay unwarranted attention to uncomplimentary nicknames and to the whisperings and snickerings of groups of youth in their presence. There is some indication, by way of the emphasis that is placed on youth in advertising, that adults may be envious of the adolescent and desire to be like him by copying his fads, manners, or dress. One seldom sees a mature person displayed in invitations to buy. The accent is on youth and the appeal is toward erasing the years. To document this phenomenon one need go no further than to note the lengthening of hair styles and tightening of trousers among the adult males of the late 1960s or the shortened skirts and the colorless make-up of their female counterparts, all fashions which began in the adolescent world.

Negative attitudes flow from feelings of conflict, ridicule, rejection and envy. Thus, there is evidence that many an adult looks upon the adolescent with hostility and perhaps with a good bit of fear and dislike. It is not acceptable, however, in our society, for an adult to openly express these negative emotions. We, therefore, often find a contradiction of feelings and action among adults. As Friedenburg puts it, "In today's society, they will probably have to be nice to the kids despite their fear and hostility but they will most certainly try to maintain by seduction and manipulation the dominance they previously achieved by coercion and punishment."[3] Margaret Mead is quoted as saying: "Teenagers are the current scapegoats for adult apathy, indifference, lack of imagination." An anonymous mother said to Judge Mary Conway Kohler: "You ought to bury them at 12 and dig them up at 18."

A totally different point of view is held by other adults, who look upon the adolescent as the bearer of all that is good. He is considered to be wiser concerning social practices, more ethical, and more understanding of what is right for the human race than his elders. These adults are the self-appointed defenders of youth as well as the self-appointed critics of their own generation. They call attention to the honesty of the former vis-a-vis the compromise of the latter. They see bravery in rebellion, spiritual goodness in experimentation, and beauty in strange (to adult ears) combinations of sounds and words. To them, the adolescent embodies courage, idealism, and is seen in some measure as being a searcher for the Holy Grail, the one who retrieves the torch dropped from weary adult hands.

Adults can be described as looking upon adolescents in two entirely different ways and there is something true as well as something false in the bipolar ideas. Despite their divergence, such ideas may from time to time be held in sequence by one adult considering one adolescent. Certainly, most who deal with this age group show some ambivalence, some oscillation in

[3]Edgar Z. Friedenberg, *The Vanishing Adolescent* (Boston: Beacon Press, 1962), p. 7. (Reprinted by permission of the Beacon Press, Copyright © 1959, 1964 by Edgar Z. Friedenberg.)

attitude, just as the youths being considered fluctuate in their behavior.

This kind of adult vacillation can be understood and may even be condoned, but there is another attitude held by adults toward adolescents which seems unpardonable. Douvan and Adelson aptly describe this image as "the fool."[4] In speaking of the adolescent, they say:

> He would ordinarily be imagined as a figure of fun— callow, flighty, silly, given to infatuations, wild enthusiasms, transient moodiness. Prototypes: Andy Hardy, Henry Aldrich. . . . The Fool exists outside the world of adult happenings: He is blessedly innocent of complication, guilt, or responsibility. He is a fool not in being duped, but because he is not yet related to the intrigues and corruptions, or the moral seriousness of adulthood.

In other words, this kind of attitude on the part of adults relegates the adolescent to a position of being less than a person. He is seen as a two-dimensional puppet of capricious action rather than as a person whose behavior, according to his style of development, is as much goal-oriented as at any other age.

An adult who cannot accept the adolescent as a developing person seeking self-realization in his own way and at his own pace is incapable of providing counsel.

What Is the Adolescent Really Like?

In attempting to describe what counseling is, the authors have outlined certain areas about which all counselors agree. Underlying each of these is the necessity for empathy on the part of the counselor, for understanding the counselee as a person, for entering into his world. Now that we have given some idea of the varying ways in which adults may view adolescents, we shall try to take a look at what the adolescent as a person really is like. How can we, as adults, really enter into his world?

Accepted Generalizations   Actually, there is no way in which the printed word can establish understanding of the counselee as a *person*, just as there is no way to be sure that the above

---

[4] Elizabeth Douvan and Joseph Adelson, *The Adolescent Experience* (New York: John Wiley & Sons, Inc., 1966), p. 1.

remarks about adult attitude toward the adolescent describe any particular adult's point of view. Unfortunately, then, we have to resort to generalizations—always a questionable procedure when what we really want is to understand a particular person.

The first generalization, as a warning about what follows, is that there is no such thing as "the adolescent." Rather, there are unique individual persons who are passing through a series of years which our society has chosen to call *adolescence.* We do not have to even roughly designate the years. We can simply say that these are the people whom you teach. We can further say that you must understand them as well as you can because what they need by way of counseling will be derived from the kinds of people that they are.

As an introductory exercise for developing an understanding of the adolescent's need for counseling, we would invite you to look at yourself as you were three, five, ten, or fifteen years ago. We do this in spite of the fact that the process may be painful and indeed, despite the fact that some theorists describe a specific amnesia for adolescence. According to this theory, one can remember the events of adolescence, but without their emotional intensity.[5] It appears to us that understanding can be enhanced by a recall of events even if the accompanying emotions are, in retrospect, blander than they were in actuality. We can still say to you: "Look back. How did you feel? What did you want? What did you fear? What embarrassed you? What were you ashamed of? What made you proud? What made you angry? What made you happy? Did anyone understand you? Who did you talk to? Could you talk to any adults? Why, or why not? What were they like?"

One of the authors issued a similar invitation to a recent meeting of parents of adolescents. In order to set the mood for an introspective glance into the past, popular music which was current during their adolescent years was played. The surprising result was that the parents were able to realize many of their own adolescent feelings and to find them quite similar to those of their children. Most of you have the asset of being close enough to your own adolescent years to utilize this as one method of understanding. There are, of course, limits to this method of introspection and reflection. Teachers generally spent their ado-

[5]Anna Freud, "Adolescence," in *Recent Developments in Psychoanalytic Child Therapy,* ed. Joseph Weinrib (New York, International Universities Press, Inc., 1960), p. 6.

lescent years in different economic and social circumstances from many of their students. Teachers tended to be better motivated toward learning and to enjoy more success at school. Nonetheless, an honest look at your adolescent years may help to increase awareness as to the character of today's adolescents.

A more obvious method of increasing understanding of students in the secondary schools is to turn to the literature which describes general adolescent characteristics and behavior. Unfortunately there are fewer points of agreement among researchers and theorists than we might like to find. After reviewing most of the theoretical positions applicable to present-day thinking about this period of time, Muuss, is able to find agreement about the following points: sexual characteristics, body image, and cultural transition.[6]

Theorists agree that there is endocrinological change with its concomittant affect on primary and secondary sexual characteristics. An increase in sex interest, awareness, and desire causes behavioral changes. The adolescent, then, finds that he must learn to regulate a new biological drive.

During this period, there is a change in the individual's body image. For the first time, he begins to see himself as he will look throughout his life. He is sometimes plagued by voice change and acne. Differences in his body contours appear. He may be early or late in his physical maturing. Either condition has an effect on his concept of his body.

Theorists agree that adolescence is a definite period, a transition between childhood and adulthood. The period begins with the physical changes of being accepted and accepting oneself as an adult. Earlier maturing of girls is recognized. Pubescence is experienced by the female from ages ten to fourteen; by the male from eleven to sixteen. There are individual and cultural differences regarding the onset and end of the adolescent period. Adolescence can be experienced in many different ways. During this period, there is a greater disposition to emotional and social difficulties. At the same time, there is a clearer definition of past and future, fantasy is better separated from reality and there is a re-evaluation of both social and psychological relationships.

In addition to the points of agreement which Muuss outlines, certain other impressions about adolescents are generally accepted. One idea is that of the affluence of the teenager. In

[6]Rolf E. Muuss, *Theories of Adolescence* (New York: Random House, Inc., 1962), pp. 159–65.

November, 1966, the NBC "Today" show quoted statistics which indicated that adolescents control about 16 billion dollars of the country's wealth and estimated that the control would be extended to some 20 billion by 1970. Much of this money is spent on extras rather than necessities. Boys heavily purchase gasoline and clothes, and spend money on hobbies, dating, and entertainment. Girls buy clothes, beauty products, and jewelry. The teenager is sought after as a consumer of goods and is wooed by designers and advertisers.

A Time for Decisions   Another generally accepted truth is that, in our society, the adolescent is pressured for decisions which to a large extent will control certain aspects of his life for as long as he lives. Vocational choices and/or educational decisions which influence vocational choices must be made during these years. Super has demonstrated that many such choices have to be made by ninth-grade boys, well before they are actually mature enough to act with wisdom.[7] Neither the educational system nor society provides much assistance for the boy who makes the wrong choice. Even the student who wants to become a dropout at 16 has, in most states, full legal sanction.

Those who stay in school have to decide to make a record which will allow either advanced or terminal education. Incidentally, this applies not only to scholastic endeavors but to social behavior as well. In the latter area, the decision may be whether to exert one's individuality or to recline upon the Procrustean bed of the successful college applicant. The high school student of today knows that admissions officers consider not only his scholastic performance but also his participation in other school affairs, his social acceptability, and his goals, as well as his ability to obtain recommendations from members of the academic organization. In these matters his chances of acceptance depend to a large extent on his early decision to project the expected image of a member of the student body at the college of his choice.

In present-day society, the male adolescent must make decisions concerning military service, the complications of which would test the wisdom of most adults. Following are just some of the ways of meeting one's military obligations other than

[7]Donald E. Super and Phoebe L. Overstreet, *The Vocational Maturity of Ninth-Grade Boys* (New York: Bureau of Publications, Teachers College, Columbia University, 1960), pp. 149–58.

that of simply waiting to be drafted. One may choose to enlist in any one of the five branches of the armed services. Each of the armed services also has available enlistment in organized reserve units. Although enlistment procedures are the same for all the services, programs of each branch differ in length of time required and in opportunities for selecting training and assignments. In addition, two of the services offer enlistment in the National Guard. Adding to the complications of the young male's decision are the opportunities for earning commissions as officers which vary according to his level of education and the institution which he attends.

The female adolescent, and some males as well, must make decisions about marriage. Fifty percent of the female population marry while in their teens, and some of them remain in high school, as do their husbands. Indeed, in some states, it is legal for children of 12, 13, and 14 to marry.[8] Whether or not a female actually marries in her teens, she makes decisions during these years about her behavior, her education, and her career which may make a difference in her opportunity or desire for marriage at a later date.

Acquiring Self-Identity   Many authorities also view the age of adolescence as a time when a person necessarily acquires self-identity. Erikson describes the primary developmental task of adolescence as being a search for identity.[9] The search is not easy in a society in which the adolescent has to choose between acceptable contradictions, and one which also keeps the adolescent "bound under a monolithic authority structure in one of the few remaining unfree (and thus irresponsible) roles."[10] The adolescent is subject to a society in which adults maintain poverty in the presence of affluence, grow rich on war material while they cry for peace, indulge in public sexual titillation and pass laws on obscenity; these among other discontinuities. Sometime during the years of his youth the adolescent must cease to be a child who can, and indeed is expected to, accept adult dicta without question. He must become, at least in basic character-

---

[8]William S. Kephart, "Legal and Procedural Aspects of Marriage and Divorce," in *Handbook of Marriage and the Family*, ed. H. T. Christensen (Skokie, Ill.: Rand-McNally & Co., 1964).

[9]E. H. Erickson, *Childhood and Society* (New York: W. W. Norton & Company, Inc., 1950).

[10]James S. Coleman, *Adolescents and the Schools* (New York: Basic Books, Inc., Publishers, 1965), p. viii.

istics, an adult who has come to terms with his unique possibilities for shaping a life satisfactory to him in a society which offers innumerable differing potentialities. He must separate himself from the security offered by conformity to parental and other authoritative adult figures. He must come to terms with an ambiguous society, and this without really knowing the rules. The adolescent leaves the world of childhood with its fairly obvious system of cause and effect, punishment and reward, and enters a situation where trial and error, as a course of action, predominates. He has to shape his own way if he is to become truly adult.

Entrance into the adolescent period can be compared with the experience of a person who comes into a darkened house. The house is completely wired and electric light is available in all the rooms. But the person doesn't know which switches turn on what lights. An outsider who cares for this person may wish that he could furnish a wiring plan. But for this house, he doesn't have one. Thus, the only way that the lights can be turned on is to allow a certain percentage of error in finding the switches. The person in the house, like the adolescent in search of himself, must try and fail, try and succeed, and finally come to know where the switches are so that the lights may be turned on. He tests his actions against some standard. In the case of the person in the darkened house, the standard of course, is the production of light.

Different Views of the Adolescent   Two observers of the adolescent scene, both popular and prolific writers, are James S. Coleman and Edgar Friedenberg. Both have engaged in extensive empirical studies of the adolescent and, interestingly enough, they arrive at differing descriptions of his status in modern society.

Coleman describes the adolescent as living in a subculture which is quite distinct from the adult world.[11] He makes the statement that "This world is increasingly becoming a world apart with adolescent goals ill understood by adults and adult goals ill understood by adolescents." Coleman says that the adolescent culture is shifting its interests further and further away from academic achievement and describes its members as being "nonchalant toward scholastic matters, irresponsible, and hedonistic." Values, ideas, interests, and attitudes are shaped by the

[11]Coleman, *Adolescents and the Schools*, p. vi.

peer group. It is more important for the adolescent to "belong" than to exercise autonomy. He is punished by his peers if he steps out of line. For instance, Coleman speaks of a major conflict as that between not working too hard in school (avoiding being a "curve raiser") and being one of the fellows, and being unpopular. Coleman thinks that the place of the adult in influencing the adolescent is to direct values already possessed by his subculture (such as competiveness) toward adult goals. If this were done the adolescent might increasingly become immersed in subcultural activities. Coleman's ideas raise some questions. Would not the result tend to widen the break between adult society and adolescent society? Would not cross-societal communication diminish? Would not adult direction finally be replaced by adolescent-chosen goals?

Coleman further believes that the energies of the adolescent subculture can be directed by responsible education toward outcomes desirable to the school. He thinks that the school can use the values inherent in the subculture and the desire of the adolescent to maintain these values for educative purposes. He suggests that adults can successfully contribute to the education of the adolescent only to the extent that they are sensitive to the influence of the peer groups. The teenager as described by Coleman seems destined to become more and more differentiated from adult society and less and less able to indulge in cross-societal communication. In addition, the adolescent may experience much emotional strain from social competition within his subculture.

Friedenberg found adolescents to be amazingly conforming to the expectations of adult society.[12] He sees the adult world as successfully manipulating the teenager by rewarding him for conformity and punishing him for expressions of individuality. The adult world has its own picture of the "successful" adolescent and it allows little deviation from this image. Thus, all but the most courageous of adolescents are pressured into conformity and there is no allowance for conflict between the generations. To Friedenberg, this means that adolescence, as such, is ceasing to be, since he defines the period as one of conflict. His idea is that a period of conflict *must* be available to the teenager if maturity is to be achieved. For failing to provide such experience, Friedenberg indicts most of the adults who are closely

[12]Edgar Z. Friedenberg, *Coming of Age in America: Growth and Acquiescence* (New York: Random House, Inc., 1965).

associated with youth: parents, teachers, and school counselors as well. Actually, we find some agreement in the positions taken by Coleman and Friedenberg in that both emphasize the tendency of the adolescent to conform either to the customs of the teenage subculture or to adult expectations.

A third current opinion regarding the adolescent experience is offered by Douvan and Adelson.[13] Their conclusions, based upon empirical study, also offer some challenge to previous conceptions. Perhaps the most original contribution of these workers is their emphasis on the importance of sex differences in modifying the adolescent years. In orientation toward the future, boys are primarily concerned with work and preparation for successful accomplishment. This makes them nonrealistic about possibilities for upward mobility, more inclined to seek detachment from the family, more inclined to participate in gang-like groups and to see these groups as a modifier of behavior. Girls, on the other hand, are oriented to the future in terms of marriage. They are concerned with interpersonal skills, indicate more fantasy in considering mobility, show little desire for less parental contact and are likely to make two-person rather than group relationships. The authors stress the point that the adolescent years for boys and girls differ in almost every respect: Boys gain adult sexuality by separation from the father; girls through identification with the mother. While boys seem to follow Erickson's order of the "eight stages of man" by occupying themselves with the task of achieving identity in puberty and adolescence followed by the achievement of intimacy in young adulthood, girls appear to reverse the order.

> Out of her intimate connections to others, through processes of identification and projection, the woman comes to know her own individuality and to solve the question of who she is. . . . The fact is that in our culture at least the need to marry and find acceptance and love exert such pressure on the young girl that we can hardly imagine her having the time and energy to invest in indentity resolution until she has gained some measure of security in a stable love relationship.[14]

A second important finding by the above authors is that the model adolescent experience is the same regardless of geograph-

[13]Douvan and Adelson, *The Adolescent Experience.*
[14]Douvan and Adelson, *The Adolescent Experience*, p. 349.

ical area or social class. The model adolescent avoids conflict, appears unwilling to take psychological risks, and settles down with his parents for the endurance of a long dependency period, apparently without much overt rebellion. Thus, we find concurrence with Friedenberg's description of "vanishing adolescence."

> Traditionally, adolescence has been the age in which the child readied himself to leave home, and when we read accounts of adolescence in the earlier part of this century we very often note between father and son a decisive encounter . . . in which the son makes a determined bid for autonomy, either by leaving home, or threatening to do so, and meaning it. . . . Nowadays the adolescent and his parents are both made captive by their mutual knowledge of the adolescent's dependency. They are locked in a room with no exit, and they make the best of it by an unconscious *quid pro quo*, in which the adolescent forfeits his adolescence, and instead becomes a teenager. He keeps the peace by meeting his natural rebelliousness through transforming it into structural and defined techniques for getting on people's nerves. The passions, the restlessness, the vivacity of adolescence are partly strangled, and partly drained off in the mixed childishness and false adulthood of the adolescent culture.[15]

Most of what has been said has been deliberately pointed toward the majority of those who are in their adolescent years, the majority which makes up most of the students with whom secondary school teachers deal. There are, of course, others who deviate markedly from the norm, either while they are in high school or after they leave by dropping out or graduating. For example, there is Hersey's portrayal of John Fist, an "overachiever unlaxing" who simply awakes one morning and decides to cut his 8:10 class because "it was too far to walk," a beginning reaction to overconformity which ended in a succession of LSD trips.[16] There are those who leave home in other than traditional ways. There are the hippies, members of a subculture which appeared in early 1966 and which 18 months later numbered themselves at some 300,000 and were subjects of articles in most of the popular magazines. *Time* magazine describes them as follows:

[15]Douvan and Adelson, *The Adolescent Experience*, p. 354.
[16]John Hersey, *Too Far To Walk* (New York; Alfred A. Knopf, Inc., 1966).

> They are predominantly white, middle-class, educated
> youths, ranging in age from 17 to 25. . . . Overendowed
> with all the qualities that make their generation so en-
> gaging, perplexing, and infuriating, they are dropouts
> from a way of life that to them seems wholly oriented
> toward work, status, and power.[17]

To some of their elders, they appeared as misfits, hedonistic
and irresponsible. Others saw the hippies as seeking recognition
as individuals, as spiritually motivated crusaders for more soul
in society, as proponents of brotherly love. The hippies themselves seemed not so much in conflict with society as disaffected
by social mores and laws. Regardless of divergent adult view-
points, the movement of the middle-class adolescent into hippie-
dom certainly provided one way to leave home.

In summary, what can we say that we know about the adolescent as he really is? In some ways he is like you were but there
are differences because he lives in a different world. Undoubtedly, he experiences extensive physical changes which modify
his behavior. This was also true of you as an adolescent. But he
is richer. He is faced earlier with more complicated decisions.
He is more pressured to conform either to peer group or adult
standards and his nonconformity is more visible. But no matter
the differences, the cultural expectations of what the adolescent
period should accomplish are the same. One enters the adolescent
period as a child and is expected to emerge from it an adult.
The passage, perhaps, is no rougher now than it was then but
it is different. The individual making his way through this
period needs understanding and assistance from those who have
been before. Such understanding can be increased by means of
introspection, reports of empirical studies, and descriptions from
the public press.

Adolescents' Concerns and Need for Counseling

What can we say about the concerns and tasks of adolescents
which may be affected in a positive way by secondary teachers
and counselors? According to people who dare make predictions
about the world in which present-day adolescents will live as
adults, conditions will be vastly different from those that we now
know. Michael has indicated some of the changes which may be

---

[17]*Time* Magazine, Vol. 90, No. 1 (July 7, 1967), 18. © Time Inc., 1967.

expected over the next 20 years.[18] He mentions such possibilities as an increasing ability on the part of human beings to manipulate their behavior and their environment. He anticipates crises in labor, education, urban development; in fact in most facets of human life. Changes in occupational demand will cause job losses and retraining anxiety. We will need to reconsider the place assigned to women as far as opportunities for educational and vocational achievement go. Michael points out that the difference in vocational demand for the "haves" and the "havenots" will increase. Students will find themselves under greater pressure to choose "careers which exploit talents and aptitudes" and, therefore, they will be "more anxious, more competitive, more 'hemmed in' earlier in their education."[19]

Michael goes on to say that the next 20 years will bring about a confusion of values. We will find more conflict between our national interests and the interests of the total world. We will become more and more likely to subject individual needs to those of a planned society. Because of the premium placed upon highly trained and superior abilities, there will be a growing tendency to allow the few of the more privileged to look after the many of the less privileged. Michael closes his prediction with these words:

> What, then, is an appropriate philosophy for guiding youth into the kind of world we have speculated on? . . . If we keep a vivid appreciation of the changes tomorrow may hold, and if we keep, too, a sober sense of our limited capacity to influence the trends involved, we ought at least to be able to plan more realistically for youth. . . . In particular—we must explore—which of the values and goals that we hold dear are appropriate to inculcate in youth for living in tomorrow's world.[20]

It must be apparent to those who have been young or involved with youth during the decade of the Sixties that much of what Donald Michael indicated in 1963 has already come to pass. In our present dealings with the adults of the 1970s and 1980s we must keep aware of these changes.

There is more to come. As an illustration of the kind of world

[18]Donald W. Michael, *The Next Generation* (New York: Alfred A. Knopf, Inc., 1963), p. 185.
[19]Michael, *The Next Generation*, p. 192.
[20]Michael, *The Next Generation*, pp. 192, 193.

which the adolescents whom you now teach will face, we refer
to ideas presented in 1967 by Augenstein concerning the relationship between technical advances in biophysics and ethical
issues.[21] He said that the next generation will certainly be faced
with these major decisions: the use of techniques to manipulate
the working of the mind, the use of "spare parts" to keep people
alive almost indefinitely, and how to deal with the population
explosion. But even more astonishing is the fact that man is on
the brink of being able to manipulate his genes so as to blueprint
through chromosomatic structure what *kinds* of human beings
shall be allowed life. This biotechnique will make *man* the decision maker as to what man is to be. It is a fact that the adolescent of today will be faced with questions like these: Who shall
be allowed to conceive children? What kind of children shall be
allowed life in our society? Who shall make decisions like these
and on what basis?

The above description of the world of the future may indicate
some of the things which adolescents *should* be concerned about
and with which adult counselors might help. When we turn to
the literature, we find the adolescent described as having concerns about such things as his physical image, exclusion from
or status within the peer group, his future either in an occupational field or marriage, relationships with friends of the same
or opposite sex, his educational progress and knowledge about
"the right" college, and obtaining freedom from parental authority.

Self-reports, however, indicate that the concerns of adolescents
may have a slightly different emphasis. A few months ago, one
of the authors had the opportunity of reading something like
100 autobiographies written by high school seniors.[22] The concerns reflected in these papers were of two classifications, per-
sonal-social and eductional-vocational. More of the former than
the latter were indicated. The students wrote about being shy,
moody, jealous, unsure of themselves, fearful of being hurt, and
feeling unimportant to other people. In their relations with
adults, they mentioned nagging parents. A remarkable number
of them disliked their teachers. Financial concerns were mentioned but most of these teenagers were solving that problem

[21]Leroy G. Augenstein, "Social Responsibility, Imperative for Interaction," *Journal of Home Economics*, Vol. 59, No. 8 (October, 1967), 629–
35.

[22]By courtesy of Dr. Audrey Riker, Consulting Psychologist, West
Lafayette, Ind.

by taking on part-time jobs. In speaking of educational matters, they remarked that classes were boring, that teachers wasted too much time and that they couldn't force themselves to concentrate on their studies.

Although the concerns listed are not by any means all which the young people expressed, they are illustrative of the fact that these adolescents appeared to be concerned with the here and now rather than the future. To the extent that a similar condition exists widely, there may be a "credibility gap" between adolescents' concerns and adults' concepts of what the adolescent should be concerned about. Or it may be that communication between generations is so poor that the elders actually are unable to understand the thinking of the younger groups. Teenage panel members on the NBC "Today" program recognized the gap in communication by expressions such as the following: Parents are afraid of the power of the teenager. They don't know the answers for which teenagers are looking. Parents are allowing rather than understanding. They tell us, "Have a good time, but don't bother me." There is no such thing as growing old gracefully. Everybody is trying to be a teenager.

Included in the remarks by the young people was the idea that adults should have dignity and not be apologetic. The adolescents said that they wanted authority, "someone who is stable, not crazy like we are." All this seems to indicate that the adolescent is much concerned about the lack of ability to communicate with adults.

If responsible adults are to get at the real concerns of adolescents, then they must come to accept that ways of perceiving the world other than the adult way are profitable. The adult's way is not necessarily *the* way. Culkin cites McLuhan's ideas about difficulty in cross-cultural communication.[23] There are cultures that are so far apart in perception as to cause intercultural abrasion. Members of different cultures perceive things through different goggles provided by the culture. People who wish to communicate must be aware of this. Communication does not consist in saying things, but rather in having things heard. You have to speak in the language of the audience. You have to know what values they value. You have to be aware of their style of life. The essence of learning about what really concerns adolescents, then, is to hear them. One student said about his coun-

[23]John M. Culkin, "A Schoolman's Guide to Marshall McLuhan," *Saturday Review* (March 18, 1967).

selor, "He doesn't like my problems." You, the teacher who counsels, must *listen*, learn to hear your students' problems, and respond to them.

"To listen" sounds easy but it is rare, indeed, to find a person who is skilled in this art. It is even rarer to find an adult who can listen to an adolescent. At this point, the reader might like to review what has been written about listening in the previous chapter. He may find it helpful in understanding the adolescent to think back over his own life and to determine the number of times when he has been really listened to as he has expressed his concerns. He may be interested to know that the most often repeated phrase in adolescents' evaluation of their experience in being counseled by counselor-trainees is, "I liked it because I had someone to listen to what I wanted to say." True listening appears to be the major factor in the establishment of understanding between adults and adolescents.

SUMMARY

It is possible to describe the adolescent in present-day society and appraise his behavior now. It is possible to project his short-term future and decide what preparation he should be making now, insofar as this projection can be extended. His present concerns can be listed as he decides them. All these factors indicate in some measure possible areas in which counseling may be needed. This is all that can be said. For when a particular adolescent relates in a counseling way to a particular adult, the only germane concerns are those of *that* young person. He alone can tell about his need for counseling. He alone can indicate his concerns. The challenge is to make this kind of communication possible by respectful and egalitarian listening. It is difficult to open oneself to cross-cultural experience. Seeing through the goggles of another is not easy. Neither is it impossible if we are honestly concerned that the young people who are intrusted to us receive counsel with wisdom. And the adolescents in our high schools are indeed asking in many ways for wise counseling, and often want to turn to the adults whom they see daily in the schools.

SUGGESTED READINGS

The following books are paperbacks. Each of them offers fairly easy and very interesting reading to the teacher who wishes to update his knowledge of adolescent behavior; he will possibly find that concepts about adolescence have changed considerably since he studied the subject in school. The following references reflect the changes and point to further modification in the future.

Committee on Adolescence, Group for the Advancement of Psychiatry, *Normal Adolescence*. New York: Charles Scribner's Sons, 1968.

Erikson, Erik H., ed. *The Challenge of Youth*. Anchor Books Edition. Garden City, N.Y.: Doubleday & Company, Inc., 1965.

Josselyn, Irene M., *The Adolescent and His World*. New York: Family Service Association of America, 1952. This early "classic" is included because of its many forward-looking statements. It should be interesting to the teacher of the 1960s who experienced adolescence in the 1950s.

Muuss, Rolf E., *Theories of Adolescence*. New York: Random House, Inc., 1962.

PART TWO

The Teacher as Counselor

Part One has set the framework of guidance and counseling in the schools. Part Two will give specific attention, with examples and role-playing situations, to the counseling responsibilities of teachers.

Not everyone believes that teachers can or ought to enter into counseling relationships with their students. Chapter 4 takes the position that these relationships are inevitable for good teachers. In the following chapters, situations calling for counseling by teachers are discussed and methods of approach to these situations described. Counseling approaches and understandings appropriate to various group situations are also described. An effective helping relationship, whether parent-child, counselor-counselee, or teacher-student, calls for certain personal characteristics. What is known and not known about these characteristics is discussed in the last chapter with special reference to the teacher who counsels.

4

A Teacher's Role

With an understanding of what to expect of school counselors and of what counseling is, we proceed to the teacher and his counseling encounters with students, both as individuals and in groups.

Teachers, as they talk with students about their concerns, are indeed counseling. Of course, counseling is not their main activity—teaching is. But good teachers cannot and do not stay uninvolved with the concerns of individual students. Good classroom teaching will result as students come to see their teachers individually, bringing with them their problems and concerns. Thoughtful counseling with these students will enhance classroom teaching for all. Teachers who listen to their students, who show clear concern for them, not just as students but as people, and who let students know them will enjoy their teaching more and will often be better teachers. Teacher and student become more understanding of each other's problems and points of view. One teacher, near retirement age, became involved in a homeroom guidance program. After initial unease in this new relationship to students, she told the school counselor that it was the first time she had ever enjoyed teaching!

Some books on guidance and counseling disagree with this point of view. They take the stand that, although teachers talk with individual students, these conversations or conferences should not be called counseling because counseling is a difficult, complex skill which requires special training. Ohlsen suggests to teachers how they should set up private conferences with students who want to talk with them with the goal of trying ". . . to help the normal child who is temporarily bothered by a problem to understand himself better, and to discover ways of coping with his difficulty."[1] However, he does not want this kind of conference to be called counseling.

Arbuckle is also reluctant to have teachers counsel but for different reasons.[2] He agrees that teachers do not have enough training but carries the argument further to say that teachers' basic responsibility is to the school rather than to individual children and that teachers, by the nature of their job, are separated from counseling. As authority figures, as people who are instructing, directing, and judging they find it hard to assume the listening, accepting, and understanding role of the counselor. Arbuckle strongly questions teaching experience as a prerequisite to school counseling; he sees teachers as necessarily possessing traits that work against good counseling.

Glanz is unconcerned about whether what a teacher does when he talks with a student is called counseling or not.[3] "Many teachers," he says, "unaware of the fact that they are not counselors, have continued to talk with students and to be involved with them in solving problems of all types." They cannot help but be counselors.

Whether teachers talk, counsel, or hold private conferences with their students, they do have contacts with individual students. These contacts should be as useful as possible. Though untrained as counselors, many teachers are of inestimable help to students who bring their concerns to them. Indeed, some

---

[1]Merle M. Ohlsen, *Guidance Services in the Modern School* (New York: Harcourt, Brace & World, Inc., 1964), pp. 417–18.

[2]Dugald S. Arbuckle, *Counseling: Philosophy, Theory and Practice* (Boston: Allyn & Bacon, Inc., 1965), pp. 188–90.

[3]Edward C. Glanz, *Foundations and Principles of Guidance* (Boston: Allyn & Bacon, Inc., 1964), p. 297.

studies suggest that counselors with very little training can be as effective as highly trained counselors.[4]

Why Teachers Counsel

First and foremost, it is an inescapable part of a teacher's job to counsel with his students. He may not need to talk individually with most of his students, but in order to reach many of them, he must learn more about them. In part, he can learn more from students' cumulative records. But records do not disclose the kinds of information about a student that come from personal knowledge of him. Moreover records are often incomplete and most secondary teachers are too busy to make full use of them. By knowing more about some hard-to-reach students, teachers may then know how to teach and how to deal with these students so that they can benefit maximally from the classroom. One teacher in talking with a boy whose work had suddenly declined discovered that the boy's father was dying. The boy was up half the night nursing him. Knowing the situation, the teacher was able to adapt class assignments so that the boy could keep up with his work.

Teachers normally ask students who are having trouble with their work to stay after school or come in during a free period. Some of these students just need a little extra help. Others need to be understood by the teacher. Why does John rarely or never bring in his homework? Why does Mary pay so little attention in class that she is a "psychological truant?" Why is Anita absent so much that she is always behind in her work? Teachers who take the time to *listen* to students' points of view often understand their behavior better and are then better able to help them learn.

Teachers find that they cannot help all the students with whom they seek to counsel. It is easy to say that they should then refer such students for help, but this is not so easy to do. The boy

[4]Zunker, Vernon G., and Brown, William F., "Comparative Effectiveness of Student and Professional Counselors," *Personnel and Guidance Journal,* Vol. 44 No. 7 (March, 1966), 738–43. Robert R. Carkhuff, "Differential Functioning of Lay and Professional Helpers," *Journal of Counseling Psychology,* Vol. 13, 117–26. T. M. Magoon and J. E. Golann, "Non-traditionally Trained Women as Mental Health Counselors/Psychotherapists," *Personnel and Guidance Journal,* Vol. 44, 788–93.

whose father is dying may need more help than one teacher can give him but may not want to talk with anyone else. It takes counseling skill on the part of the teacher to help some students become willing to see a school counselor and be receptive to such counseling. Future counseling or therapy will be most effective if the teacher is able to prepare the student for help from the school counselor or other specialist. Merely asking the counselor to call in a student is asking him to counsel an unwilling student. Doing so without first asking permission of the student is also breaking confidence with the student.

Teachers have frequent occasion, also, to talk with parents whose children either are not doing well in school or are behaving in ways unacceptable to the teacher. To refer to parent conferences as counseling is clearly unjustified when teachers confine their remarks to listing the shortcomings of the students under discussion. But when teachers take the time and have the respect to listen to what parents can tell them about their children, and to work with parents to help them understand the behavior of their children so that their school experiences will be enriched, then counseling can take place. Teachers and parents both are apt to be uncomfortable when they come together. Knowledge of counseling can help teachers be more at ease when parents come in and to counsel and *listen* rather than tell, advise, or berate.

Talking with or counseling with individual students and parents gives teachers an opportunity to know their students better. This knowledge makes it easier for teachers to teach some students they otherwise might not be able to reach. Teachers who know their students are able to develop closer relationships with their classes which enable them to be more effective teachers. A teacher who had been having trouble with her classes became interested through the school counselor in one or two underachieving students. Coming to know these students better helped her to see others in the class as individuals. Students who had been complaining about her reported that her classes were much better, and the teacher reported the same change.

Evidence is growing to show that more learning actually takes place in a trusting, accepting atmosphere than in a harsh, unaccepting atmosphere. Our own experience reminds us that we have usually learned more with teachers we have liked and/or respected. With enough need to learn, it is possible to learn from almost anyone. Students in our secondary school classrooms are not usually motivated to this extent. Some recent studies lend support, if not directly to the idea of a favorable environment, then to the idea that a teacher who is able to relate well with other people is more effective. Carkhuff and Berenson cite studies which show that teachers functioning at a high level of interpersonal effectiveness have enabled students to grow as much as two and a half years in school achievement in one school year as compared with six months' growth in achievement with teachers functioning at a low level of interpersonal effectiveness.[5]

Even in group situations many teachers can develop counseling relationships. They are often expected to assume group guidance or homeroom guidance responsibilities as part of their teaching load. They are expected to be an adviser to students in their homerooms, come to know them well, and involve them in group discussions of common adolescent problems. Those group guidance programs which have been successful have provided teachers with the help of specialists in working with informal groups of this kind and have also provided them with time to prepare for this added responsibility. Teachers are often involved in other informal groups of students as they serve as club advisers or chaperone dances. Some teachers, as an aspect of their subject matter, conduct discussions which center around values and behaviors as part of teaching about certain literary works, particular eras in history, or current events. Courses or units in psychology, personal relations, intergroup understandings, and family living involve counseling. Some subject matter may relate directly to a student's concerns. For example, conflict and violence as a theme in history may be relevant to a student involved in personal conflict, violence, or rebellion. Teachers can use subject matter to help students understand some of their concerns about themselves and the world.

Teachers counsel, then, because it is part of their job to know their students in such a way as to help them learn more, to listen to and understand students as part of developing a healthy relationship with their classes, as part of their course content, and lastly because students come to them for help. Just because the teacher is an adult and is there, students will come to him for help.

When we have talked with high school students, we have asked them to whom in the school they would go if they had a

[5]Robert R. Carkhuff and Bernard G. Berenson, *Beyond Counseling and Therapy* (New York: Holt, Rinehart & Winston, Inc., 1967), p. 14.

personal problem. Most of them replied that they would go to a teacher. When asked why, they have responded that their teachers know them better than their counselors, which confirms what has been said earlier about adolescents' need to establish good relationships with some adults and *to be known* as a person. Many of us remember teachers to whom we have taken our concerns and problems, both large and small. Students come to teachers for help in their work and end up talking about their problems. They ask for help in vocational decisions and college choices. They look for understanding when they break off with a "steady." They want their teachers to know them and they feel that they can trust teachers enough to talk with them about themselves.

Some teachers are especially sought out by students. Teachers of subjects such as physical education and home economics see students less formally than most other teachers. These teachers and others who have found students coming to them with problems often look for courses in counseling so that they will be more competent in helping students with their problems.

Pitfalls For Teachers Who Counsel

Convinced though we are that teachers counsel as part of their jobs, there are, nonetheless, cautions which should be noted. Teachers can counsel but they must know not only how to refer but when and whom to refer. They must be careful not to take on counseling which demands more time and skill than they have to offer. There may be students with whom teachers could work if they did not have responsibility for teaching 100 other students. *Counseling is part of their job only as long as it supports their teaching.* They may also encounter students whose problems are so severe that someone whose main job it is to counsel should be the one to help, with, of course, the interest and support of the teacher. In the next chapter, there will be chances to consider some of the problems in knowing whether or not to refer a student, some of the same problems that Mrs. Howe was considering at the beginning of the book.

The position that teaching is too different a function from counseling for teachers to be able to counsel is not without merit. To counsel, many teachers have to unlearn habits and attitudes that have been with them since they started teaching. A counselor accepts, though not necessarily agrees, with what he hears.

He listens. A teacher must judge, evaluate, and discipline. He corrects some of what he hears and may have to reject inaccurate statements of students. He finds it hard to listen to complaints about the school or about his fellow teachers because he is so much a part of the school and feels that he must defend it.

A counselor holds what he hears in confidence, though he too may often be torn between his commitment to the individual and his loyalty to the school. How much harder for the teacher to maintain confidence if he has been told about some behavior that is against school regulations! Like the counselor, he must make judgments about the extent of confidentiality which he can maintain. Knowing that he is more limited than the counselor in guaranteeing confidentiality, he should not offer more confidentiality to a student than he can give. A teacher in whom a student confides should warn the student if he feels that he must report certain irregularities to school authorities.

In supervising beginning counselors, drawn from the ranks of teachers, we often say to one, "You sound like a teacher." When we point this out, our novice counselors are able to see how they have interposed a didactic response, such as, "Why don't you try? What's preventing you?" or "I'm sure that your science teacher really isn't that bad." Didactic responses such as the above can be appropriate, but not if they indicate rejection of what has been said, or reflect real lack of empathy. Teachers can learn to be counselors but they often have to make some changes. They can learn to shift from one role to another, from the one who must keep order in the classroom to the one who listens and understands. Students understand this dual role. One student approached a teacher who was supervising in the lunchroom. He started to ask her something and then said, "You have to be strict now, don't you? I'll see you after school."

Teachers can learn to use more of a counseling approach in their classrooms in leading discussions and as a valuable tool in handling some discipline problems. Effective teachers have little trouble shifting roles.

Role Playing

The chapters which follow will discuss in more detail some of the counseling problems of teachers, give illustrations from real experience, and suggest role-playing situations, both for individual and group situations. Role playing is an excellent procedure for learning about counseling. Before presenting situations, an explanation of what role playing is and how it can be used is in order.

Participants in role playing take the role, or position, of someone in a particular situation which, for our purposes, is a counseling situation. They begin either with a situation given to them or with a familiar situation which they would like to try out. The participants take some time first to examine the situation and think about how they would handle it or respond. They need to know enough about the role they are playing to play it intelligently; that is, they must either have some background information or develop some. When they begin to play their roles, they play them as realistically as possible, beginning with the counselee knocking at the door or in whatever way is appropriate to the situation.

Role playing can take place in privacy, or before a class, or in small groups within a class. If before a group, it becomes a learning situation for everyone. The group, or class, needs to remember that role playing is not a performance and therefore to refrain from laughing or other comment. The role players need to remember the same thing. If they really play their roles, they will forget the class and be completely absorbed in the role playing. The intent of role playing is for the role player to feel and act like the person whose role he is playing. In so doing, he gains understanding of that person. In role playing a counselor, he has a chance to practice counseling and to begin to feel like a counselor. In role playing a counselee, he has a chance to understand how a student feels who brings his problem to a teacher or who is sent to a counselor and how a student reacts to different counseling approaches.

In role playing, the situation is rarely played out to its conclusion but rather a time sample is taken. The role players begin and continue for maybe five or ten minutes until they or the instructor or the class decide the role playing has gone far enough so that it can be discussed. When role playing concludes, the participants talk about how they felt, why they said what they did, how they reacted to what was said to them, etc. If presented before a class, the class usually enters into the discussion.

The value of role playing, for our purposes, depends on thoughtful preparation of the participants, real involvement in the roles, and especially on the thoughtfulness of the discussion which follows the role playing. Discussion under the direction of the class instructor or other leader will typically consider such things as the feelings and reactions of the participants, the reason for the choice of responses made, the possible consequences of alternative responses, and the counseling approach being used.[6]

Role-playing situations can be easily developed from the experience of people in a class, experiences they have had as students or as teachers.[7] One person thinks of a situation he remembers where he, or someone he knows, was not sure of the best counseling procedures. For example, he remembers Diane who was sent out of class for an outburst directed toward the teacher. In this particular class, the teacher had started out the year by promising the class they could choose a special field trip. Every time the class asked when they could talk about a field trip, the teacher put them off, saying they weren't ready yet. Spring came and the question came up once more and again was put off. Diane, usually quiet and reserved, burst out, "Boy, you're always putting us off. You promise and promise and don't do anything about it. I don't think you really meant it to begin with." The class applauded and Diane was sent to the principal. The principal told her she would have to apologize or be suspended. Diane, who had never been in any kind of trouble before, was both aghast and frightened but still didn't think she should have to apologize. She had only told the truth. So she turned to a teacher whom she liked and trusted.

The class or role-playing group discussed the case and asked more questions of the originator of the situation. They decided it would be a good situation to try out. They talked then about some of the considerations facing the teacher. Should he support his fellow teacher? What kind of help does Diane need? What if

[6]Fannie R. Shaftel and George Shaftel, *Role Playing for Social Values* (Englewood Cliffs, N.J.: Prentice-Hall, Inc., 1967. Although this book describes the use of role playing for a different purpose, it is extremely helpful for an understanding of role playing in general. Other books helpful to understanding role playing and role-playing procedures are Kenneth Benne and Bozidar Muntyan, *Human Relations in Curriculum Change* (New York: Dryden Press, 1951), Chapters 14 and 15, and Alan F. Klein, *How To Use Role Playing Effectively* (New York: Association Press, 1959).

[7]Role-playing situations can also be developed from case books such as Esther Lloyd-Jones, Ruth Barry, and Beverly Wolf, eds., *Case Studies in Human Relationships in Secondary School* (New York: Bureau of Publications, Teachers College, Columbia University, 1956), or Irvin Faust, *Entering Angel's World* (New York: Bureau of Publications, Teachers College, Columbia University, 1963).

he agrees with Diane? Then the role players talked about Diane. How would she be feeling? How would she show it? What did she expect of this teacher?

After this initial discussion, two members of the group volunteered to play the roles of Diane and her teacher, Mr. Young.

> *Mr. Young*:   Come in, Diane, what's on your mind?
>
> *Diane*:   Mr. Young. I'm in terrible trouble. I'm . . .
>
> *Mr. Young*:   (interrupting) You in trouble, Diane? That's not like you.
>
> *Diane*:   I know, but I am and I don't know what to do.
>
> *Mr. Young*:   What's happened?

Diane tells what happened, ending up with, "I just don't think I ought to have to apologize. I told the truth and all the class agreed with me."

> *Mr. Young*:   Well, I can see why your teacher was sort of upset.
>
> *Diane*:   I didn't mean to upset him. But if I apologize, it just wouldn't be right. I'm not sorry. I think what I said was right.
>
> *Mr. Young*:   But Diane, this isn't like you. The school just can't let people get up and tell teachers off. Don't you think you could at least tell him you're sorry you upset him?

At this point, the leader of the role-playing group called for a halt and asked Diane what her reactions had been. She said she felt frustrated, as if she couldn't get Mr. Young to understand how she felt. There was a lot she had wanted to tell him but he hadn't really given her a chance. Mr. Young said he thought Diane would have to apologize eventually so he wanted to help her understand this. He also felt he had to support the principal's decisions. One person pointed out that Mr. Young had not really listened. Another wondered if Mr. Young would support the principal's decision even if it were patently unfair to Diane.

After several minutes of this kind of discussion, one of the members said he would like to try Mr. Young. The same person played Diane.

Mr. Young: Come in, Diane, you look upset. What's happened?

Diane: Mr. Young. I'm in terrible trouble.

Diane tells what happened, ending up with, "I just don't see how I can apologize. I only told the truth."

Mr. Young: You don't see why you should have to apologize for telling the truth.

Diane: Yeah, that's it, but if I don't I'll get suspended. No one in my family has ever been suspended.

Mr. Young: It would seem like a real disgrace to get suspended but you don't want to give up what you think is right, either.

Diane: Yeah, I've been brought up to stick by what I think is right.

Again the leader of the role-playing group called a halt so that the group could discuss what had gone on thus far. Diane said that this Mr. Young came closer to understanding how she felt. She felt he was listening and trying to understand. Mr. Young said he wasn't sure how it was going to work out, but he thought that in counseling Diane he should try to see her side of it. He wanted to help her see the consequences of whatever she decided to do and support her right to make her own decision. The group discussed the differences between the two Mr. Youngs. The first Mr. Young felt obliged to support the principal's stand. The second Mr. Young felt obliged to try to help Diane in a way which would not involve taking anyone's side. Which role would have felt most comfortable to you? Why?

Role playing can lead to extended understanding of counseling, of students, of teachers' relationships to students, and even of yourselves. We hope you will take advantage of the role-playing situations in the book and develop your own as well.

Mrs. Howe and Susan—Practice in Role Playing

As an example of role playing, look again at Mrs. Howe and Susan in the Introduction. Mrs. Howe, after innocently asking Susan about her college plans, is faced with a weeping girl who has unloaded strong emotions on her. She has to say or do something to resolve the immediate situation and, hopefully, to lead to help for Susan. Whoever agrees to role play this situation should first think about it carefully. The person playing Mrs. Howe will want to consider how Mrs. Howe feels at this moment and to think about how to handle the situation. He may have to provide himself with some information. Is there a guidance counselor in the school? A school psychologist? The person playing Susan will want to consider how Susan feels, what made her unburden herself at this point, and to think herself into Susan's position as she stands weeping before Mrs. Howe.

The point in role playing this situation is not to explore the various alternatives open to Mrs. Howe in, for example, referring Susan for help but to consider the alternative responses for Mrs. Howe to use *now*. Why does she choose the responses she does? What is she trying to do? What can she say to Susan? As the situation is role played, how does Susan react to it? Does she feel rejected? understood? embarrassed? Discussion at the conclusion of role playing Mrs. Howe and Susan may lead you to ask two other role players to play the same situation, or a counselor with a different approach to role play with the same Susan.

SUMMARY

Teachers, as part of their responsibility as teachers, are involved with individual students in such a way that they must necessarily become counselors part of the time. They need to come to know their students in order to teach them better. They are regarded by students as adults with whom they can talk. In their classes and in informal groups of students, they discuss values and behaviors. Effectiveness in their counseling role will enhance their teaching and provide opportunity for closer adult-adolescent understanding.

SUGGESTED READINGS

Gordon, Ira J., *The Teacher As A Guidance Worker*. New York, Harper & Row, Publishers, 1956.
The chapter on the teacher as a counselor presents the case for the teacher functioning in this role and presents sound guidelines and cautions.

Johnston, Edgar G., Mildred Peters, and William Evraiff,

The Role of the Teacher in Guidance. Englewood Cliffs, N.J.: Prentice-Hall, Inc., 1959.
A thorough discussion of the role of the teacher in guidance. Examples of teacher counseling with students are given.

Sachs, Benjamin M., *The Student, The Interview, and The Curriculum.* Boston: Houghton Mifflin Company, 1966.
A distinctive discussion of counseling in the schools. The importance of the teacher to the student is emphasized. Taped interviews are presented and analyzed.

Strang, Ruth, and Glyn Morris, *Guidance in the Classroom.* New York: The Macmillan Company, 1954.
Written for classroom teachers, the authors discuss in simple terms the responsibilities and possibilities for teachers in guidance.

Wiley, Roy De Verl, and Melvin Dunn, *The Role of the Teacher in the Guidance Program.* Bloomington, Ill.: McKnight and McKnight Publishing Company, 1964.
The authors give a complete picture of the teacher's role in guidance, including discussion of when it is appropriate for teachers to counsel with both students and parents.

5

Gathering Information

Before teachers confer with students, whether on the
initiative of the teacher or student, they often gather
information about the student which they feel will help
them in talking intelligently and helpfully with the
student. Although the procedure of gathering information seems logical, it can be questioned. Some teachers prefer not to know too much about a student before
they talk with him for fear that they will be prejudiced by others' opinions. They feel it is hard not to
be influenced by the adverse comments of former
teachers or by a record of previous failures and hence
prefer not to examine student records until they have
formed their own judgments. Others say that as professional people they are able to evaluate objectively
available information about students without undue
influence from others' experiences. They would rather
know at the beginning of the term that a student has
just gone through a breakup of his family than make
some inadvertent remark which would hurt him. Or
knowing that a student has found English difficult in
previous years, an English teacher can be ready to

give this student extra help at the beginning of the year before he has a chance to fall behind. Still another point of view is represented by Grant who writes that, "The good teacher possesses only information about pupils which reveals ability, achievement, potential and interest. The possession of other information of a more personal nature is not necessary to teach the pupil."[1]

If a teacher seeks information he should know why he is seeking it and be able to justify its use in terms of the improvement of his teaching. The key word is *relevant*. Whatever information is gathered should be relevant to the teaching and counseling task. Contrary to Grant, we believe that information of a personal nature may be necessary to teach particular students. Awareness of a recent change in family circumstances, such as divorce or death, may help in teaching the student concerned. However, when teachers or other school personnel probe into the personal lives of students, they are exposing themselves to the charge of invasion of privacy.[2]

Those teachers who seek information beyond what they see of students in the classroom must first ask themselves what information, they want and why. They look not for just any interesting information, but for information which will help them understand why certain students are misbehaving, not doing well in their classes, or looking for counseling help. They will want to know first about ability and past achievement. It is always possible that a student has been placed in a class where he is unable to keep up with the work. Knowledge about students' interests may help teachers reach the students. Family background may help explain students' attitudes toward school. Teachers also may want to know about students' feelings about themselves which may explain unwillingness to try, lack of confidence, or trying too hard. Not every teacher would want to look for the same information about each student who presents a learning or behavior problem or who comes to him for help.

Where to Find Information

The first source of information is the teacher himself. Unless it is very early in the school year, he has observed some things

---

[1]Claude Grant, "The Teacher-Student Relationship Is Not Counseling," *Journal of Counseling Psychology*, Vol. 7, No. 2 (Summer, 1960), 149.

[2]Edward Van Allen, *The Branded Child* (New York: Reportorial Press, 1964.)

about the student and has gained some impressions. He can extend this information by making a point of watching the students with whom he is concerned. What is their behavior in class? How do they get along with others in the class? Do they behave better at some times than at others? Do they show any signs of fatigue or illness? Some teachers make a point of talking individually with each student, even if only for two or three minutes. Asking students to write something about themselves is another way of coming to know them. One teacher asked all his students to write on why they were taking his course and what their goals were. Although an assignment like this lends itself to some students writing what they think the teacher wants to hear, it nevertheless gives the teacher additional knowledge of his students. Another teacher asked his students to write three things about themselves. Reading these papers made the class come alive to him.

The guidance office is an obvious source of information. Where there is no guidance office, there are usually central student records with some relevant information on them. The school counselor or school psychologist may have helpful information not on the records and can also review the records with teachers to help them interpret what they find in the way of test scores and past achievement. Student records should contain information about relevant family background, ability, past achievement, interests, employment, and health.

Cumulative records, which often appear dull and lifeless, can be brought to life if read intelligently. Even the address can be helpful if you know the community well enough to recognize the address as one in a wealthy or ghetto part of town. The teacher reading them can raise questions: Why have his grades dropped here? What would it be like to live there? Does the fact that his mother is not living at home affect his school work? Why is there such a difference between his test scores and his grades? Is football his only outside interest? Why has he been absent so much? Is he over his illness of last year? Is there any reason why he always does poorly in this one subject? Other information must be sought in order to answer these questions.

Other teachers provide a very valuable source of information. Teachers from previous years may be helpful, as well as those who have a student now. In a small community, teachers often know a great deal about students and their families. Sometimes a student presents a problem to all his teachers, sometimes just to one or two. Talking with those to whom he presents no problem may help those to whom he is a problem. Gathering information from other teachers must, of course, be kept on a professional level. It is only proper that relevant information be shared with one's professional colleagues, but it must not degenerate into teachers-room gossip with each teacher topping the other with tales of student misdeeds. Such unconsidered talk can label a student and unduly prejudice other teachers toward him.

An often untapped source of information lies in observation of students in informal situations. Why is Jane no longer paying attention in class? She is no longer walking down the hall hand in hand with Mike, who is now walking hand in hand with Josie. The understanding teacher then knows that the situation will mend itself in time and that Jane will again be able to to pay attention in class when she finds another boyfriend. Teachers can learn about their students observing them in the hall, the cafeteria, at school games and school dances, getting on and off the bus, before class starts.

Intelligent Evaluation and Use of Information

How good is the information? Even standardized test scores are liable to errors. Because they are objective, we tend to accept them as accurate, often to the detriment of a student's welfare. All test scores are subject to a certain amount of error because test scores are only samples of what a person can do. A statistic called the *standard error of measurement* can be computed for tests to tell us what the range of error is. For example, the standard error of measurement on the verbal reasoning section of the Differential Aptitude Test is 2.8. This means that the chances are two out of three that a person's true score is somewhere within a range of 2.8 raw score points on either side of the obtained score. (In other words, the obtained score plus or minus 2.8.)[3] Teachers who understand this error will learn to look at a test score as a range or band rather than a point. In addition to this error built into the test, errors also occur as a result of individual differences at the time of test taking such as illness, discrepancies in test administration, and scoring errors.

[3]George K. Bennett, Harold G. Seashore, and Alexander O. Weswan, *Differential Aptitude Tests Manual* (New York: The Psychological Corporation, 1966.)

A notable source of error in standardized tests lies in their bias in favor of the middle class. Test items have generally been constructed on the assumption that all children have had the same experiences. We know now that this assumption is not true. Test items have assumed experiences that children from minority groups or ghetto backgrounds simply have not had. These children then have done less well on tests than children from middle or upper socioeconomic backgrounds and have then often suffered from the assumption made by their teachers that they are of low intelligence.[4] Knowing that this social class bias exists, particularly with intelligence or scholastic aptitude tests, the New York City schools no longer give tests of scholastic aptitude. Teachers working with disadvantaged populations must be especially careful in evaluating information gained from test scores.

With some understanding of the reasons why standardized test scores cannot be considered infallible, teachers can avoid the danger, described by Berdie, *et al.*, of using tests and test scores in such a way that they become ". . . the center of attention, displacing the individual with whom we should be concerned. A test score can accrue a reality of its own. Counselors and teachers sometimes use tests not much differently than fortune-tellers use cards or tea-leaf readers use teacups."[5]

Teachers should always feel free to raise questions about scores which do not make sense to them in light of what they know about a student. Test scores are clearly only *one* source of information about ability and not an infallible one. Sometimes teacher judgments are better. Sometimes past achievement is a better indication. Some combination of different sources is best: test scores, records, teacher reports, interviews, autobiographies, etc.

Always, teachers must evaluate information about students thoughtfully and consider the reliability of the source. And then, only tentative conclusions should be reached because later information may change the whole picture or the student may change. If a too firm conclusion is reached, later information may be rejected because it doesn't fit the first conclusion. For example, a teacher may be so convinced by other teachers that

[4]Allison Davis, *Intelligence and Cultural Differences* (Chicago: University of Chicago Press, 1951.)

[5]Ralph F. Berdie, Wilbur L. Layton, Edward O. Swanson, and Theda Hagenah, *Testing in Guidance and Counseling* (New York: McGraw-Hill Book Company, 1963), p. 78.

a student is unable to do the work in his class that he is unable to accept the possibility indicated by test scores that the student has more ability than he has yet evidenced in school and hence the teacher may not expect much of him, so that a self-fulfilling prophecy takes place.

Information, depending on its nature and the person receiving it, can either help or hinder a teacher in counseling a student. If the teacher responds to information that a student's mother spends all her time in the local bar by saying, "What's the use, she's just like her mother," then the information is detrimental. If he responds by trying to understand how the mother's behavior may affect the student, the information is potentially helpful. In their teaching activities, teachers gather many bits and pieces of information about students. When interested in a particular student, they can add to knowledge already gained by systematically gathering further information from the guidance office and other teachers. Such information needs to be put together carefully and objectively to help the teacher better understand the student's behavior, and then to counsel (and teach) him.

SUMMARY

A teacher, when counseling with a student, may want to gather more information about him. If so, he should think carefully about what information he wants and why. Sources of information are the guidance office, cumulative records, other teachers and informal observations. Information should be carefully evaluated. Whether or not the teacher seeks information preceding a conference with a student, he has gained some initial impressions and has some information. As he takes the role of counselor, he must try to keep the information in mind without letting it hinder his listening to what the student has to say. While he is with the student, all his attention should be on understanding what the student is trying to tell him, not in fitting new pieces of information into old.

SUGGESTED READINGS

Gibson, Robert L., and Robert E. Higgins, *Techniques of Guidance: An Approach to Pupil Analysis.* Chicago: Science Research Associates, Inc., 1966.

Helpful for teachers who want to know more about techniques of learning about students. One of several of approximately the same title which discuss these techniques in detail.

Karmel, Louis J., *Testing in Our Schools*. New York: The Macmillan Company, 1966.
Written for parents, a clear easy-to-read description of the uses of tests in schools to help students.

Lyman, Howard B., *Test Scores and What They Mean*. Englewood Cliffs, N.J., Prentice-Hall, Inc., 1963.
Helpful for the teacher who wants to understand more about test scores. Intended for readers who do not have much background in tests and measurements.

Morris, Glyn, *The High School Principal and Staff Study Youth*. New York: Bureau of Publications, Teachers College, Columbia University, 1958.
Presents clearly the need to know students as individuals and describes methods for so doing.

Tyler, Leona, *Tests and Measurements*. Englewood Cliffs, N.J.: Prentice-Hall, Inc., 1963.
Addressed to those who need to understand tests and measurements well enough to use test information correctly, but who do not wish to become experts. Clear and understandable.

6

Problems With School Work

The following chapters on counseling individual students cannot possibly present all the possible situations concerning individual students which may confront teachers. There are, of course, endless possibilities and combinations of possibilities. We can, however, divide counseling situations with individual students into categories which will make them easier to consider: academic problems, vocational-educational problems, parent conferences, and personal problems. None of these problems is ever a pure one, that is, one is always affected by another. However, the focus of counseling can be on one problem even though consideration of other concerns may be not only relevant but necessary. Examination of these problems and examples of them can lead to better teacher understanding of these problems and increased competence in dealing with them, but not to pat answers on how to cope with each problem that a student presents.

Undoubtedly, the majority of teacher conferences with individual students are occasioned by academic problems, students whose work or behavior presents a problem to the teacher. That this is so is hardly surprising since teachers' chief responsibility is promoting academic development. When they encounter students who are not progressing satisfactorily, or whose behavior disrupts their teaching, they are concerned, and rightly so. Never before has educational achievement been so important to individual development. This is especially true for students from minority groups whose ability to advance and find jobs is especially dependent on successful completion of, at the least, high school.

Special Problems of Teacher-Initiated Counseling

Counseling is appropriate when a student comes to the teacher for help with his work and also when he is asked by the teacher to see him after class or after school. The characteristics of the counseling relationship are as appropriate to conferences concerning school work as to any other interpersonal relationship. This kind of relationship makes it easier for the student to understand his own problems as they relate to school work and for the teacher to understand the student's difficulty and thus know how to deal with it. It enhances the learning climate of the classroom by making the conference a learning situation and by strengthening student-teacher relationships.

A counseling approach gives the teacher the opportunity to explore with a student the reasons for his difficulty with his work. The teacher is interested in finding out how the situation looks to the student, in listening to his side, and in helping him work things out himself. A student, in talking with an interested listener, may realize for himself that he wants to do better in class, that doing so is up to him, and that he must be more regular with his homework. In this way, he learns for himself rather than being told by the teacher. He assumes responsibility for himself rather than the teacher assuming it for him.

In listening, the teacher may learn that a student has problems which interfere with successful completion of school work. The range of such problems is great and usually not simple, that is, there is likely to be more than one thing which makes school difficult for him. Teachers can help with some problems, will need to refer others, but can always listen.

Special Problems of Teacher-Initiated Counseling

Most teachers find it uncommonly difficult to approach with an open mind a student who is doing poor work in his class. Students who are doing poorly constitute a threat to the teacher because they raise questions about his competency. Teachers may resent or be angered by students who appear indifferent to the subject matter because to them it is important and they see it as important in their students' academic development. What is more aggravating than a boy lounging in the back of the class, interested in anything but what you are trying to put over with the lesson plan you worked on so hard! Understandably teachers find it difficult to throw off resentment and enter into any kind of counseling relationship with a boy like that, but if resentment is met with resentment, little progress is made and the student is cheated of learning. If resentment is met with interest and concern, progress may be made toward improvement of the learning situation. Difficult though it may be, the only way to help that boy is to come to know him.

The fact that a teacher-initiated conference centers on a problem defined by the teacher and not by the student makes it different from the usual counseling situation. Counseling is more easily effective when it is sought by the student. However, students in academic difficulties are often asking for help in the only way they know how. Teachers who understand this tell the students what counseling has to offer them and then find many of them eager and grateful for help. Those who continue not to be receptive are often the ones most in need of help, demanding the utmost in persistence and understanding from their teachers.

One element of counseling that most counselors agree upon is the counselee's right to make his own decision. One wonders in dealing with academic problems if teachers can allow students to decide whether or not they will do homework. How much responsibility can be given to students to make their own decisions and in what areas depends on their maturity. Students can be allowed some kinds of decisions but not others. "Do you want to do your homework before or after supper?" not "Do you want to do your homework?" Adolescents have a wider range of decisions than do children. Moreover, they have reached an age where they cannot always be forced to behave as we think they ought. At some level or other, the decisions are theirs, whether we like it or not. Although we can coerce or persuade most boys to do their homework, there are some we cannot force because they do not care whether or not they fail. We can make a high school girl sit down with her books but we may find it hard to force her to really study for her tests. Nevertheless, teachers counseling students with academic problems cannot allow the range of decisions for the students to go beyond the framework of the educational restrictions in which both they and the students are operating. A social studies teacher may, in conferring with a student, allow him to choose among some different kinds of assignments, but he cannot give him the decision of whether or not to do any assignments.

How Teachers Can Help

When a student finds in a teacher an adult with whom he can talk, he may start coming to the teacher ostensibly for help with his schoolwork but actually for a chance to talk. As Kemp says, adolescents are often ". . . anxious, guilty, uneasy with nagging inferiority feelings. Some isolate themselves, feel defeated, and are unable to tell anyone."[1] A sensitive teacher will realize this and encourage the student to talk with him about his concerns and doubts. By so doing he is helping the student. It is not unusual in such cases for schoolwork to improve even though it has not been talked about or directly approached. Teachers do not ordinarily have the time to help students work through concerns about family, heterosexual relationships, or vocation, but by listening, caring, and trying to understand they can do more than they think.

Teachers can try to be sure that adolescents know the consequences of their decisions. If Tom refuses to do his homework, he will fail the course. If knowing that, he decides not to do his homework, there is little a teacher can do except to maintain a relationship with Tom so that he can come back to the teacher if he changes his mind or wants to talk about other things. If Susie decides she would rather do other things than study, then she should be helped to understand that poor grades in high

---

[1]C. Gratton Kemp, *Intangibles in Counseling* (Boston: Houghton-Mifflin Company, 1967), p. 81.

school will limit the kinds of choices she can make later about her future.

Teachers can try to find out the reasons for refusal to do homework or to study. It may be that Tom has no place to study or no time because he is helping to support his family. Susie may not study because none of her friends like school and she feels she will lose her friends if she does well in school. Understanding the reasons for behavior, teachers can usually find ways to help such as suggesting to Tom that he use the public library for studying or involving Susie in group situations with students who like school.

Stewart and Warnath, in studying academic achievement, conclude that if motivation and ability are adequate, good academic achievement is related most closely to identity development: ". . . Good academic achievement would depend on the individual's concept of himself, his goals, his perceptions of reality conditions, the strategies by which he plans to achieve his goals, and, of course, the objective conditions of his environment."[2] Anything a teacher can do, then, to help students develop positive feelings toward themselves could contribute to improved academic achievement. Giving students ample opportunity for academic success, showing that someone cares about their achievement, and helping students develop strong peer relationships are some of the ways in which teachers can help in the development of self-identity or self-concept. In addition they can help students set goals and see how academic achievement relates to these goals.

Glasser describes the feelings of delinquent adolescent girls with whom he talked. They said

> . . . that they would only go through the motions of school, that they had no hope of learning anything that would be valuable now or later in their lives. They realized that without a good education they were handicapped, but when I asked them whether they would work hard in school now that they realized the gravity of their situation, they said they would only try hard enough to pass. Having accepted school failure, they would make no effort that might lead to success in school.[3]

[2]Lawrence H. Stewart and Charles W. Warnath, *The Counselor and Society* (Boston: Houghton Mifflin Company, 1965), p. 231.

[3]William Glasser, *Schools Without Failure* (New York: Harper & Row, Publishers, 1969), p. 2.

Teachers can take the time to listen and try to understand. If they are able to see how school looks to students who are doing poorly or misbehaving, they sometimes understand and even sympathize with their behavior. For many, school is not a good place. It is rather a place where they are scolded, yelled at, derided, and experience failure, a place where they are made to feel inadequate. Nothing in it relates to their life outside the school. Students who see school this way need teachers who will listen before they can begin to respond in the classroom. Actually, most students do care about school. They don't like to do poorly. It is up to teachers and counselors to help them understand the consequences of doing poorly, and then help them find ways of improving. The student on the bottom of the academic ladder is so accustomed to failure that he sees no way up. He needs the continual concern and encouragement and faith of those around him.

EXAMPLES

Mr. March stopped Tom as he was leaving class and asked him to come in after school. Three weeks of school had gone by and Tom still had handed in no homework. When called on in class he disclaimed, almost with a sneer, any knowledge of what was going on. He managed to do this in such a way that it often drew a snicker or two from some of the other students. Mr. March wanted to talk with Tom before he asked the school counselor about him.

> *Mr. March:* Hi, Tom. Sit down over here. (Tom sat down but did not reply or look at Mr. March. Mr. March was quiet for a while trying to understand Tom's reaction. Hostility? Shyness?)

> *Mr. March:* You'd rather not be here?

> *Tom:* What d'ya mean?

> *Mr. March:* Well, I get the feeling you're not too happy being here.

> *Tom:* I'm not. What d'ya want?

> *Mr. March:* To talk with you, but I guess you don't want much to talk with me.

Tom: What about?

Mr. March: Well, let me tell you. Right now you're failing history because you're not doing the work or paying attention in class. It's early enough in the year for you to do better. If there are reasons why you're not studying or things which are making it hard for you, I'd be glad to talk about them with you. Maybe I could help. You don't have to stay now if you don't want to. If you'd like to stay and talk some, I'd like to have you. Or you can come back some other time. It's up to you.

Let's look at how another teacher might approach Tom under similar circumstances.

Mr. Winters: Hi, Tom. Sit down over here. Why aren't you handing in any of your schoolwork?

Tom: I dunno.

Mr. Winters: There must be some reason. You know that if you keep on not doing your work, you'll fail history. You don't want to fail, do you?

Tom: No.

Mr. Winters: Well, then do you think you can start doing your homework?

Tom: Yeah.

Mr. Winters: That's fine. If you do your homework, you'll know some of the answers in class. Wouldn't that be better than always saying you don't know?

Tom: Yeah.

Tom does not look up at **Mr. Winters.** He remains slouched in his seat.

Which example is best? **Mr. March** leaves the decision of whether he wants to stay up to Tom. He is not forcing him into a counseling situation but opening the door. If you are looking, in this example, for a Tom who leaves the conference full of new resolve, you are disappointed, but you must know that it rarely happens that way. It would not be realistic to bring this example to a glowing conclusion with one short after-school conference. Only a beginning can be made. How much of a beginning depends on the student and what he brings with him.

Mr. Winters has talked *to* Tom rather than *with* him. He has asked him questions such as "You don't want to fail, do you?" which admit of only one answer however insincere. He has not indicated that he is interested in listening to Tom. He has obtained Tom's agreement to start doing his homework but we wonder how real that agreement is, or if real, if Tom would be able to keep his resolve.

We like the first example best at least on paper. In theory it comes closer to the characteristics of counseling. In actuality it is hard to tell. We do not know how Mr. March and Mr. Winters said what they said. Tone of voice may convey a great deal. Mr. Winters, who sounds cold on paper, may have sounded real to Tom. In these short examples, without seeing and hearing what went on, we cannot be sure how much concern, empathy, etc., were communicated. However, Tom's failure to look up at Mr. Winters and his slouched position suggest that he was not responding favorably to Mr. Winters.

Counseling is not subtle persuasion. Mr. Winters comes closer to persuading than counseling. Counselors and teachers who counsel sometimes see counseling as persuading the student to do what he doesn't want to do without his knowing that he is being persuaded. If you want to counsel, counsel. If you want to persuade, then persuade but not under the cloak of counseling. Teachers often want to persuade. Much of their teaching is persuasion. When they see bright students not working up to capacity, they will persuade them to do better. They want to see them be successful and do well, and they know the importance of a student's school record to future progress, college acceptance, and job opportunities. In the following role-playing situations, see if you can counsel without persuading. Some background is given for both student and teacher.

ROLE-PLAYING SITUATIONS

1.   One way to examine the differences between the two previous examples would be to role play both teachers. Let the same person play the role of Tom, and then ask him with whom he felt more comfortable and why. With either teacher, did he feel his attitude toward the class might change? Role playing can start with the dialog given and continue where it left off. You can also try other approaches with Tom.

2.   Read the situation described below and then discuss the

approach that the teacher might use. What does she hope to accomplish in the first situation? How should she go about it? You might also want to elaborate more on Susie's role. Then choose volunteers to play the roles and give them a little time to think about how they plan to play these roles.

As in the preceding role-playing situation, follow the role playing with discussions. How did Susie feel? Did she think the teacher was listening to her? How did the teacher feel? Did he understand Susie better? Did he accomplish what he had hoped to?

> *The Teacher*:   You are an English teacher in senior high school. You have become increasingly irritated by Susie's frequent absences and lateness. Usually her work is careless and sloppy but occasionally she hands in some excellent work. You know that the art teacher believes Susie has revealed artistic ability. In looking at her cumulative record, you see that her intelligence test scores are in the 90th percentile. Achievement test scores are similarly high.

> You want to talk to Susie after school because you are sure she could be doing much better work.

> *The Student*:   You are a high school student who baby-sits regularly on school nights in order to help pay the bills at home. Your father has deserted the family. Your mother finds occasional work. You and your sister pay most of the bills. You love art and would like to go to art school.

SUMMARY

Problems of counseling with students who have academic problems are far from exhausted. There just is not space nor would it even be possible to catalog the many kinds of students with academic problems and the difficulties encountered in counseling with them. There is an infinite number of combinations. The boy whose mother is dying and who stays up late caring for her; the girl of average ability who is ignored by her parents; the ghetto student who sees no hope; the boy who wants a car and a job more than he wants school. There is no key to counseling with these students other than to remember what counseling is, and to remember that the *way* you counsel has to do with *who* you are. If you are genuine, if you can accept students who appear to be different from you, then you are well on the way to counseling with these students and helping them toward a better experience in school. School should not be a drag for students; it should not be a miserable experience with continued failure. For many it is. By counseling with them, by learning from them ways in which you can make your teaching more relevant to them, you can help them benefit more from their school experience.

SUGGESTED READINGS

Drews, Elizabeth M., ed., *Guidance for the Academically Talented Student*. Washington, D.C., National Education Association of the United States, 1961.
Discusses ways for counselors to work with academically talented students. Many of the suggestions can be adapted for teacher use.

Glasser, William, *Schools Without Failure*. New York: Harper & Row, Publishers, 1969.
Places the blame for the development of failure identities on the school, saying that schools are designed for failure. Should be required reading for all teachers.

Stewart, Lawrence H., and Charles F. Warnath, *The Counselor and Society*. Boston: Houghton Mifflin Company, 1965.
In Chapter Nine, a fine discussion of the variables in academic achievement.

7

Decisions about Education
and Careers

Of concern to most high school students are questions
concerning their vocational future. What will I be?
What am I good for? Can I succeed? Where can I get
into college? Is there a place in the world of work for
me? Where can I get a job? Will I be discriminated
against? Of more immediate concern are related questions. What language? How much science? What will
this course do to my grade point average? Will this
prepare me for a job? Will there be job opportunities
in this trade?

These are concerns with which school counselors are
prepared to work, using their counseling skills, knowledge about testing, and information about colleges and
employment opportunities. Any well equipped guidance
office will have occupational and college files with up-
to-date information available to students and teachers.
Teachers will often want to refer students to their
counselors for help with vocational-educational concerns.

Some schools, however, do not have school counselors
or guidance offices. Some have school counselors who

are not well enough prepared to deal effectively with these student concerns. Still other schools use their school counselors so poorly that the counselors spend their time with clerical tasks and have little time left to talk with students, especially those who are not planning on college. In all schools, there are students who will stop to talk with a favorite teacher to ask his opinion about jobs, college, and the future in general. Teachers therefore should have some knowledge of how to deal with these crucial concerns of high school students.

Vocational Development

How did you become a person who is planning on being a high school teacher? Pondering this question a bit will help you understand the complexities involved in *vocational development*, the term used to describe the course of one's progress from school into the world of work. When did you first think of becoming a teacher? What factors and people influenced your choice? What other possibilities have you considered? Is this a first choice or a compromise? Are you sure now that teaching is what you want? Take some time to think about these and related questions and discuss them with your friends.

Occupational choice is more than matching one's abilities and interests with those demanded by a particular job. We have known for a long time that more than interests and abilities are involved in occupational choice, but we have known very little of the process by which choices are made. In the last ten years or so, a number of scholars have developed theories of vocational development. We have chosen Super's as one which is usable and easily understood.

Super regards vocational development as part of general development.[1] Choosing and entering into an occupation, i.e., finding one's life work, are part of becoming what one is. Super describes stages through which most people go as part of vocational development. Children go through a stage of fantasizing about occupations. They see themselves as policemen, presidents, TV stars, cowboys, space pilots, etc. In adolescence comes a period of exploration. Adolescents are developing a self-concept and testing it against various possible choices. They try out

[1]Donald E. Super, *The Psychology of Careers* (New York: Harper & Row, Publishers, 1957). See also Donald E. Super, R. Starishevsky, N. Matlin, and J. P. Jordaan, *Career Development: Self-Concept Theory* (New York: College Entrance Examination Board, 1963.)

interests, consider possibilities, and think about themselves in terms of who they are and what they can be. Going from school to work is a period of reality testing, of comparing choices with the way things really are. For many people, early work history is a period of floundering in attempting to implement their self-concept, that is, to find work which seems to fit their idea of themselves. Following this period of floundering and trial comes the period of establishment when self-concept is modified and implemented. One becomes established in an occupation. In the period of maintenance, one maintains oneself in his chosen work and progresses within it. And finally come the years of decline when one adjusts to the effects of aging and the coming of retirement from work.

Not all people follow this pattern. Some know from the time they are eight what they want to be and work steadily in that direction. Some change occupations in mid-career. Many women enter a career, leave it during the family-raising period, and then return to the same or different career while others follow the dual career pattern of home and work. But the general pattern remains useful for those working with secondary school students in trying to understand what to expect of them in the way of vocational decision making.

Vocational Decision Making for Adolescents

Making a vocational decision is a process, not a point in time. There is no one point at which a high school student decides what he is going to be. His education, family background, interests, abilities, aspirations, and feelings about himself all contribute to the decision, tentative at first and then either changing to other tentative decisions or staying firm. There are of course points at which the adolescent has to make decisions pertaining to occupational choice: whether or not to take the business course, whether or not to apply for a particular job, whether or not to go to college. But these decisions are contingent upon what has gone before. They are also contingent upon the information and opportunities available at the moment to the student faced with a decision.

Let us look at a ninth-grade girl faced, as are many ninth-graders, with the decision of whether to take the academic or some other program. In some schools, the die is almost cast at this time. The student opting for a business course will have a hard time meeting college requirements should he later change his mind. Other schools have more flexible curriculums so that the decision, though still important, is not as crucial. This girl, whom we shall call Nancy, must make at least a tentative decision in ninth grade whether or not she wishes to attend college. Her decision depends in part on family background such as finances and attitudes toward education for girls. It depends too on Nancy's knowledge about career opportunities. She may be aware of few choices for women beyond teaching, secretarial work, and nursing, so that she might decide on the business course because she does not want to be a teacher or a nurse. Unaware of financial aid available for college, she might decide against college because of her family's limited financial resources.

Knowledge about herself, too, affects this decision. Nancy may believe that she does not have the ability for college or the disposition to be an office worker. On the other hand, she may have abilities and interests which would make a business course appear reasonable but cannot see herself in the business course because her friends are all college-bound or because her family expects her to attend college.

Family, social, psychological, and economic factors enter into Nancy's decision whether to take the college or business course. The decision is further influenced by Nancy's information about her interests and aptitudes, opportunities for women, college entrance requirements, financial aid to college, and school curriculum. Other high school students reach similar decision points where their decisions are affected by many of the same factors. Furthermore, each decision they make limits the range of later decisions. The boy who elects to take a vocational course greatly lessens the likelihood that he will ever attend college.

Special Problems of Minority Group Students   We like to think that every high school student can choose freely the occupation he would like to enter. However, freedom of choice is limited by the factors we have enumerated. A boy from a professional family has little chance of becoming a mechanic unless his family is very understanding. Students from the lower classes, from minority groups, and from the disadvantaged population may have their choices even more severely limited. Until recently Negroes could not aspire to many occupations unless they were unusually talented, and still find certain directions virtually closed to them. They continue to find discrimination at many levels during the process of vocational development. Children living in either rural or urban slum areas often receive inferior education and see less of the world than their more advantaged peers. Those who see the adults around them living on welfare may have no idea of what work is or that it is something desirable or possible for them.

Too much attention to what teachers perceive as reality can be particularly damaging to students from disadvantaged or minority group populations. Already with low aspirations, they often have these aspirations confirmed by their teachers who, with good intentions, point out that job opportunities are few for people from their background. Worse, teachers may assume that students from poor backgrounds cannot succeed in high-level occupations. A woman who is now a highly respected and successful professional person was placed without being consulted in a business course when she was in high school. One of her teachers, aghast at this placement, insisted that this able student take courses which would enable her to go to college.

The problem of effective vocational-educational counseling with minority group students is especially clear when white teachers or counselors are working with Negro students. A Negro professor writes:

> Sometimes motivated by prejudice, sometimes motivated by a desire to inform the Negro pupil of the "real" world he faces and of his limited opportunities to pursue occupational goals, the white counselor is discouraging and defeatist. On many occasions I have heard white counselors tell Negro youngsters that they had better set their sights a little lower, that certain professions or certain college choices are unrealistic. Malcolm X wrote in his autobiography how much as a young boy he had wanted to be a lawyer. He further related how a white teacher whom he trusted and respected crushed him by declaring that he'd better abandon thoughts about the legal profession and prepare instead for a more appropriate job as a carpenter or plumber.[2]

A study of 15-year-old Negro boys in Harlem disclosed that these boys had middle-class occupational aspirations.[3] Teachers

[2]Donald Hugh Smith, "The White Counselor in the Negro Slum School," *The School Counselor* Vol. 14, No. 5 (May, 1967), 269.

[3]Robert A. Dentler, Bernard Mackler, and Mary Ellen Warshauer, eds., *The Urban R's* (New York: Published for The Center for Urban Education, Frederick A. Praeger, Inc., 1967), p. 223.

must be especially thoughtful when discussing vocational-educational aspirations with Negro adolescents (or other adolescents who came from cultures different from theirs.) White teachers should be particularly sensitive to the hurt which Negro students have often sustained, the prejudice and barriers they have encountered, and consequent mistrust they have of all white people including teachers.

Students from these backgrounds require from counselors and teachers understanding of the different world of values in which they live. Hoppock points out that counselors, and presumably teachers, who come with middle-class values and see middle-class opportunities are sometimes disillusioned when their counselees do not respond to what appear to them to be attractive possibilities.[4] He suggests that a counselor listen as much as he talks to these counselees and their parents in order to ". . . learn some of the economic and family and cultural influences which lead his clients to do things that sometimes appear incomprehensible to members of other cultures." For many of these adolescents, choice is a luxury denied to them. Getting a job which will bring in money is their first consideration.

We are again reminded that listening is an essential part of counseling, here necessary in order to begin to understand how the world of work and entry into it look to students coming from cultures and values and perspectives different from our own.

Listening and understanding are important, but Williamson calls for counselors to do more than care for individual clients. He writes that counselors have a heavy responsibility ". . . to work diligently for the restructuring of society, local and national, so that human potentialities of all members may be more fully utilized both in the interest of each and in the interest of all."[5] Teachers also have this responsibility.

Pressures for Decision Making   A high school junior came to see one of the authors. "I have a problem I've just got to talk to you about," she said, tears welling up in her eyes. "All my friends know what they want to be but I don't know yet." A mother talking with a school counselor about her tenth-grade son said, "I'm so worried about him. He still doesn't know what he wants to be."

[4]Robert Hoppock, *Occupational Information*, 3rd ed. (New York: McGraw-Hill Book Company, 1967), p. 103.
[5]E. G. Williamson, *Vocational Counseling* (New York: McGraw-Hill Book Company, 1965), p. 43.

If adolescence is a period of exploration about occupational choice, then there ought not to be this kind of pressure on adolescents and their parents. We know that adolescence is not the time when firm choices are made. We have evidence that ninth-graders are not ready or able to make choices.[6] Yet high school students are pushed to make decisions bearing on their vocational future not only through the decisions they have to make about courses and programs but by pressure from adults.

When you were in high school, how many times did someone ask you what you wanted to be? How did this question make you feel? Asked enough times, high school students often feel they have to give some definite answer, if only to keep the adults quiet for a while. An answer given this way is of course not a real answer, nor a thoughtful one, yet it can come to be a real answer because the student begins to feel committed to what he has said. Bell tells of a junior high school student who said he wanted to be a nuclear physicist.[7] His family and teachers were delighted. He was a good student so the choice did not seem unreasonable. He prepared a talk on nuclear physics. His parents proudly told their friends that their son was going to be a physicist. It was not until he reached college that he was forced to reconsider his decision because of difficulty with some college science courses. By this time, it was a real threat to everything he thought about himself to face what appeared to him to be failure and to begin to look for alternatives to his decision to be a nuclear physicist. No one had helped him when in high school to explore other possibilities.

Asking a student what he wants to be in such a way that he feels he ought to have an answer puts undue pressure on him to make a decision without sufficient thought and all too often with insufficient help and information. Taking the answer he gives you as a final one can commit him to a direction before he is ready. In addition, the choices students must make about courses, programs, and colleges force them to early decisions.

Decisions which will affect a person's entire future ought to be made carefully. School counselors are trained to help students know how to make vocational decisions. They listen to students who want to talk and explore. They have information available.

[6]Donald E. Super and Phoebe L. Overstreet, *The Vocational Maturity of Ninth Grade Boys* (New York: Bureau of Publications, Teachers College, Columbia University, 1960).

[7]Hugh M. Bell, "Ego-Involvement in Vocational Decisions," *Personnel and Guidance Journal*, Vol. 38, No. 9 (May, 1960), 732-36.

They help them consider alternatives, open up new directions, and know how to go about implementing their tentative choices. In the near future, school counselors will be showing students how to use computerized information systems to help them in vocational decision making. If they are good counselors, they do all they can to keep choices open as long as possible and to remove pressures which schools put on students to make decisions before they are ready. Teachers can help in this process.

Planning for Post-High-School Education   In making vocational decisions, high school students have to consider the kind and amount of education beyond high school necessary for entry into the occupation they are considering. They must also make judgments concerning their ability to complete the necessary education. One high school senior with the ability to complete college and medical school finally decided against a career in medicine because she did not want to remain dependent on her parents for such a long time. In her case—and in many others—ability is not the only factor in considering post-high-school education; desire and motivation are equally important. To an increasing extent, school counselors are learning that ability is only part of college success.[8]

Post-high-school education includes not only all types of colleges, including the community colleges which are increasingly popular, but also business schools, trade schools, apprenticeships, and on-the-job training. School guidance offices should have information about these different opportunities on hand. Soon, a great part of this information will be centralized in information retrieval systems. The vast and changing amount of information about post-high-school education is more than school counselors can be expected to cope with without automated aid.

In suburban and some urban high schools, students come under unusual pressures concerning college decision and choice. Social and family pressure takes away from them the decision whether or not to attend college. They *must*. They are deprived of the opportunity to really consider thoughtfully how college fits into their plans. The only question for them becomes: What acceptable college can I get into? Students are pressured toward prestige colleges and therefore deprived of the opportunity to

[8]Morris I. Stein, *Personality Measures in Admissions: Antecedent and Personality Factors as Predictors of College Success* (New York: College Entrance Examination Board, 1963).

think about what they are looking for in a college and where they would not only get the most appropriate education for them but also the most enjoyable.

How Teachers Can Help

Armed with some knowledge about how vocational decisions are made, teachers can support counselors in helping students *keep their choices open*, widen their vocational horizons, and consider alternatives. They can help answer some of the students' many questions. Where a question is purely for information such as the requirements for a particular occupation, teachers can give the answers if they are sure they know them. Otherwise they can refer students to the school counselors. They can tell students of their own experiences and reactions to jobs they have held.

When a student asks, "What do you think I ought to do?" no one can really tell him. What we know about counseling helps. We cannot make another person's decision for him. We can help him think about it, explore possibilities, look for information, and weigh consequences, but we cannot tell him what to do.

High school students often consult their teachers about the education needed for the career they are considering as well as about college choice. Teachers can help their students think about the different kinds of post-high-school opportunities available. Where they have particular information about colleges or schools they can share it. Vocational teachers often have up-to-date information about apprenticeships. Teachers just out of college can tell students what college is like, giving them information which is not available in college bulletins but which is important to a student thinking about college. Science teachers can tell students what kind of education is needed for various careers in science. All teachers can be careful that they give only information which is accurate and refer students to the guidance office for further information.

EXAMPLES

Mr. Wilkins is a mathematics teacher talking with an eleventh-grade boy, Bob, who has dropped in after school just to talk.

Bob: You know, I've been thinking. I like math a lot and

I'd sort of like to be an engineer. My uncle's an engineer and has told me something about it.

Mr. Wilkins: That sounds like a pretty good idea. You *are* doing well in math. It seems to me that you'd have the ability there. What kind of engineer were you thinking of?

Bob: Electrical. I've looked it up some.

Mr. Wilkins: Good. You've been thinking about it some. Have you looked into colleges at all?

Mr. Wilkins has taken Bob's tentative remark as a real choice and is moving him in the direction of engineering. If the choice is indeed a real one, no harm is done, but Mr. Wilkins has not tried to find out how much thinking Bob has done about other possibilities. Mrs. Nowinski approaches a conference like this differently.

Bob: You know, I've been thinking. I like math a lot and I'd sort of like to be an engineer. My uncle's an engineer and has told me something about it.

Mrs. Nowinski: What is there about engineering that appeals to you?

Bob: Well, as I said, I like math, and I like the work my uncle does. I like working with things and figuring them out.

Mrs. Nowinski: Uh huh. Well, you do need math for engineering and you're doing well. There are other things you could do that would need math, too, besides engineering. Had you thought of any others? Like working with computers?

Bob: Well, I had thought about it some.

Mrs. Nowinski could go on to suggest how Bob could find out about other careers in math. She might also find that he enjoyed English too. In talking, it might develop that there were several other possibilities he had considered and should explore.

A different kind of problem occurs when a student mentions a career possibility which seems to the teacher to be out of reach. A ninth-grade girl doing barely passing work says she wants to be a doctor. Debbie is talking with her social studies teacher, Mrs. Gottlieb.

Mrs. Gottlieb: You want to be a doctor? But Debbie, you'd have to do much better in school. You'd have to go to college and then take four more years after that. You can't be a doctor.

Debbie: I don't care. That's what I want to be.

What Mrs. Gottlieb has said is true. It takes years of hard work to be a doctor. It does indeed seem unlikely that Debbie could be a doctor. However, Mrs. Gottlieb cannot know for sure. In trying to keep Debbie from later disappointment, she has crushed her without giving her any alternatives. Mr. Schreiner tries to help Debbie think about her future without making a firm decision yet.

Mr. Schreiner: What makes you think about being a doctor, Debbie?

Debbie: I like to help people. I've visited in the hospital and seen doctors.

Mr. Schreiner: You'd like to do something where you'd be helping people, is that it?

Debbie: Well, partly. I'd like to help people, but not if they were too sick.

Mr. Schreiner: Then maybe you wouldn't like to be a doctor. They have to see some pretty sick people. There are other jobs where you could take care of old people, or work in hospitals where you aren't with patients all the time. You can find out more from your guidance counselor. What kinds of things do you like to do? What are you interested in?

From here, Mr. Schreiner may help Debbie think of some different possibilities. He has not said she cannot be a doctor, but in listening to her he has learned that her interest in being a doctor is really not very strong. Instead of squashing her idea, he has moved on to open up alternatives.

Someone once said that if everyone had taken counselors' and teachers' advice, there would be a shortage of artists, musicians, and perhaps scientists. One can always cite famous people who did poorly in school and for whom teachers had surely not predicted a famous career. In the name of being realistic, adults often shatter adolescents' dreams. A high school student who wants to be a professional musician needs to know that not everyone who aspires to such will succeed even though he shows talent. But he can be allowed to cherish his dream, know what it entails, and work toward it if after thought and exploration it remains what he wants. It is not doing a student a favor to shield him from possible failure in the future. Moreover, we cannot be sure that he cannot succeed. He may be the one.

ROLE-PLAYING SITUATIONS

1.   Before trying this role-playing situation, take some time to discuss the special problems involved when a white teacher counsels with a black student. What feelings may the student have? How may school look to her? What should the teacher consider before talking with the student? If it is appropriate to your particular situation, you can change the student or teacher role so that some other minority group is represented.

The Teacher: You are a business education teacher. You have noticed Jackie in your typing class because she seems more interested and alert than most of the other girls in class. She follows instructions carefully and promptly. You have wondered if she belongs in this class of vocational students and have asked her to stop in and see you after school.

The Student: You are a tenth-grade student in business courses because your school counselor said it was the best place for you. You live with your mother and several brothers and sisters in a ghetto area. You do not have a father. Your mother has always worked and is usually too tired to talk much with you about school although she has always said that school is important. You are worried about why Miss Harper, your typing teacher wants to see you.

2.   This role-playing situation is about a boy who is not sure he wants to go to college. What pressures are there on boys to attend college? How should college decisions be made? Do all good students have an obligation to attend college?

The Teacher: Larry has stopped in to see you after school. You know him as a likable, able student in your advanced class. He often stops in after school with other students and chats. This time he has waited until the other students left. He says, "Mr. Miller, I don't really want to go to college."

The Student: You are an eleventh-grade student in advanced classes. You are on the basketball team, you study three or four hours every night. Your parents and teachers assume you will get a scholarship to a good college. You are beginning to feel pushed by everyone but yourself and have been thinking of just taking off somewhere after high school in order to think about what you want. You want to talk to someone about your feelings.

SUMMARY

Meeting students every day in class, and sometimes after school, teachers are often able to identify a student who seems to be in a particular course or taking a particular direction more by accident or mistake than by design. A teacher is in a better position than the school counselor to notice these students and then to bring them to the attention of the counselors or talk with them himself.

Adolescence is a crucial time in the process of vocational development. Self-concepts are firmed up and decisions made that determine much of the rest of a person's life. Though no decision is completely irreversible, many are nearly so. To reverse them may mean years of extra study or of doing without. Adolescents need all the help they can get in making wise choices, in thinking carefully about their future, and in considering alternatives. Teachers can help them in this thinking. They can also be instrumental in opening up new horizons for them not only in individual conferences but through class work.

What one thinks of oneself is formed in part by how others see one. Teachers who are positive and encouraging can enhance self-concept so that their students feel they can aspire to higher goals than they might otherwise. Teachers who denigrate students can contribute to low self-concepts which limit students' hopes and goals. Teachers are a potent force in vocational development.

SUGGESTED READINGS

From High School to College, Papers Presented at the Work Conferences on Guidance for School-College Transition,

August 17–28, 1964, at Teachers College, Columbia University. New York: College Entrance Examination Board, 1965.
Papers concerning college admissions, characteristics, and success. Interesting to classroom teachers who teach college-bound students.

Gannon, Frederick B., *The Many Faces of Kevin Michael Pullen*. New York: College Entrance Examination Board, 1968. A case study of a boy's counseling through high school leading up to a college decision. The case is then followed on through high school. An interesting glimpse of what did and did not go into one college decision.

Herr, Edwin L., and Stanley H. Cramer, *Guidance of the College-Bound*. New York, Appleton-Century-Crofts, 1968.
A clear and soundly based discussion of colleges and the college-bound.

Hoppock, Robert, *Occupational Information*, 3rd ed. New York: McGraw-Hill Book Company, 1967.
Solid background and practical help on the use of occupational information. Readers will also find summaries of most of the current theories of vocational choice.

Peters, Herman J., and James C. Hansen, eds., *Vocational Guidance and Career Development*. New York: The Macmillan Company, 1966.
Selected readings illustrating problems and important developments in the field of vocational guidance. Many articles of interest to teachers as well as counselors.

Reiss, Jean, and Mildred G. Fox, *Guiding the Future College Student*. Englewood Cliffs, N.J. Prentice-Hall, Inc., 1968.
Explores the entire role of the school in college guidance, including that of the teacher.

8

Students Have Parents

All teachers talk with parents, sometimes willingly, often with reluctance. However regarded by teachers, teacher-parent conferences are an accepted part of teachers' responsibilities. School and home together are massive influences on the lives of high school students. What goes on in the classroom can be more effective if teachers understand what parents want for their children, how they look at education, and what kind of influence they have on their children. Classroom effectiveness is helped too if parents understand what the school is trying to do and what individual teachers are trying to teach their children. Where the goals and values of school and home are in opposition much time is wasted in the educational process. Without belaboring the point that teacher-parent conferences are important, let us just say that free, open communication between parents and teachers enhances teaching effectiveness.

Secondary school teachers generally see little of parents except in school districts where pressures for educational success are very high. In these districts, parents come to the school frequently with queries about their children's progress, grades, probability of college success, and, where there is homogeneous grouping, class placement. In most high schools, however, parents infrequently ask to see teachers. Their children have reached the age where they do not want their parents to come to school as they did during the elementary school years. Yet the need for parent-teacher understanding continues. High school teachers who have effective parent conferences find them helpful in working with some students.

Teachers who prefer not to see parents are often the ones who are not sure how to talk with parents, somewhat afraid of them, and on the defensive. Knowing a little about counseling and about some of the problems in talking with parents can help teachers be more comfortable with parent conferences.

Parents and Teachers are Scared of Each Other

One of the authors was enthusiastically telling a class of graduate students, all of whom were teachers, of the many ways to involve parents more at the high school level. Carried away with the glories of better parent-teacher communications, she failed at first to notice the rather cold response of the class. When she became aware of the lack of interest, she asked if they would rather not have parents around. The affirmative answer was unanimous and heartfelt. The ensuing discussion suggested that these teachers did not want parents interfering with what they were doing. They resented time given to parents with complaints, and they wanted the school administration to protect them from parents. Later on in the discussion, the author asked how many in the class were parents. Nearly everyone in the class raised his hand. Did they as parents want free access to the teachers of their children? Yes! Indeed they did! Faced with their dual personalities as teachers who did not want to see parents and parents who did want to see teachers, the class members went on to discuss some of the reasons for this conflict.

On the teacher's side, parents are viewed as people who cause trouble. They are potential threats. They may complain to the principal if they don't think the teacher is treating their darling properly. They raise questions about how the school is functioning. They organize committees to investigate school practices. Some of them have influence. They are on the school board. They are college professors who may know more about the subject matter than the teacher. They think teachers have no one to teach except their children. Viewing parents in this way, teachers are understandably on the defensive when parents come to see them.

On the parent's side, teachers are viewed as people who have a great deal of influence on their children. They are potential threats in that they may take the children away from the parents. They give them new ideas, sometimes at variance with those at home. They teach things that weren't taught when parents went to school. They can do so much for their children or they can do so little for them in an age where school is increasingly necessary for success. They know a lot and may be critical of the home situation. Parents fear that if they complain the teacher will punish their child. Viewing teachers in this way, parents too are understandably on the defensive when they go to see teachers.

Parents are often suspicious of what goes on in the classroom. Their adolescent children bring them little satisfactory information about school.

How was your English test?

OK.

What are you studying in social studies?

I dunno. Nothing much.

Naturally, parents turn to teachers and other school officials for help in understanding what is going on. Parents who seem to be bringing complaints are often just asking for information and reassurance that their child is getting along all right and that the teacher is interested in him.

Parents Care

Any discussion among teachers about parents will bring the comment, "They just don't care about Johnny" or "The ones you really need to see never come to school." Most parents care very deeply. They may not show it in ways which are familiar to us. They may do foolish things because they care so much, but they do want the best for their children. They want them to grow up to be successful and happy. The parent who is up at the school every week does care. The parent who is overly strict does care. The parent who allows too much freedom does care.

One of the authors encountered a parent who had stormed into the principal's office more than once. The last time the prinpical managed to be somewhere else so that the angry mother was shown into the counselor's office. The mother listed her complaints about the school and her son, giving the author permission to hit her son whenever necessary. "Do you think he's happy?" the counselor asked. The mother's face changed from anger to sadness. "No." Then the mother was able to talk about her deep concern for her son. Left a widow several years before, she had to place her son in a foster home until she could care for him. Happily remarried now, she was able to provide a good home but in her anxiety to do the right thing by her son she was antagonizing him and his teachers. She cared.

"The ones you really need to see never come to school." The truth of this often heard statement can be demonstrated but it does not follow that these parents do not care. Parents of students who give the most trouble in school, whose work is poor, or whose behavior is disruptive, are not usually the ones who come to Open School Night or who ask for conferences with teachers. Even when school officials ask these parents to come to school for a conference, they receive no reply. Feeling that they have done all they can to reach the parents, they give up and say that the parents do not care.

The story of one parent who came in to see a school counselor can help us begin to understand some of the reasons why some parents do not come to school. The school sent three letters home to this father telling him that his son, who had been suspended, would not be readmitted to school until the father came to school for a conference with the assistant principal. When the father finally arrived at the school he had obviously fortified himself with a little drink before he came. "I hope you don't think I'm drunk," he said, "but I had a hard time getting up my nerve to come. I never got along very well in school myself and I'm just plain scared of schools." The counselor was then able to understand the parent's previous lack of response and to begin to work with him to help his son.

Teachers like school. They were usually good students themselves. School was important to them. To many, it is a revelation that there are adults whose school experiences were so painful and full of failure that they dread entering a school even now that they have children of their own in school. They have no pleasant associations with school or teachers. They forsee nothing pleasant in going to school now. Very likely, they will hear unpleasant things about their children. It is small wonder that many parents are loath to attend school functions or conferences with teachers.

For parents of disadvantaged children, this fear of school is particularly marked. In school, they had been denigrated and pushed around. Their clothes were not as good as those of other children. They rarely received approval and were often scolded for reasons they did not always understand. Yet they were required to attend. School represented authority. They may be self-conscious now about their dress, their speech, their lack of education. But they do care. They want their children to get an education so that they can have a better life than their parents.

Many parents are unable to come to school. Working mothers are not always able to take time off from their jobs for school conferences, concerned as they might be about their children. Mothers of preschool children cannot always find someone with whom to leave them while they go to school to see a teacher. A widow operating a small store by herself cannot leave it during store hours which extend far beyond school hours.

It is up to schools—and teachers—to find ways of reaching parents who care but are unable for any of a variety of reasons to come to school for conferences with the teachers of their children. Home visits by a counselor or school social worker can set the stage for later visits to the school by parents. Guidance departments can set up evening hours for counseling. Sometimes conferences held away from the school in a neutral setting such as a community building are successful. Though uncommon at the secondary school level, teachers can profitably make occasional home visits.

Another comment one hears about parents from teachers is, "She thinks anything her child does is all right." Meeting 100 students a day, teachers find this attitude hard to understand if not downright irritating. However, we should be able to understand that parents find it hard to be objective about their own children. In fact, we would not think much of parents who are not at least a little prejudiced in favor of their children.

Two-Way Communication

One of the characteristics of good counseling is empathy, entering into the world of another person to see how it looks to him.

Empathy requires listening. If communication is to go both ways between parent and teacher, teachers must learn *to listen and to hear* what parents are trying to tell them. They must listen for the anxiety, the concern, the fear that parents may be trying to communicate. They must try to understand the different background and values that parents bring with them, values which may be alien to those of the teacher.

In counseling, one person is engaged in trying to help another person work through his problems and concerns. Although communication of necessity flows both ways, one person is seen as the helper. In parent-teacher conferences, both parties can be described as helper. The teacher can help the parent understand school policies and procedures. He can and should bring to the parent objective information such as grades, test scores, and work samples that will help the parent understand his child. He can listen to the parent's problems and concerns. On the other hand, the parent can bring information to the teacher that may help the teacher understand the student better and hence how to teach him. Parents do know things about their own children which can be helpful to teachers. They can even offer suggestions about best ways of dealing with their child. Communication and help goes in both directions.

Teachers have often seen their role in teacher-parent conferences as that of expert. They feel they are expected to have the answers and to tell the parent what to do. Beginning teachers often say, "I didn't know what to tell her." The answer to that is to *tell* her nothing except for objective information. The teacher does not need to feel he is the authority who knows the right things to do for all children. These conferences should be cooperative endeavors. Together, teacher and parent can sometimes find solutions to vexing learning and behavior problems. When they are unable to do so, they have school and community resources upon which to call. This approach, besides being a logical one, assures the parent that the teacher is as concerned as he about his child. Parents, especially those in urban and suburban areas where teachers are not usually part of the community, find it difficult to believe that teachers are truly concerned about their children. In smaller communities parents and teachers see each other outside the school situation in the supermarket, the church, the gas station, or the local political meeting. They know each other as people before the time comes to talk about Johnny and Susan.

All that goes into good counseling can help teachers have good parent conferences, ones in which both teacher and parents leave feeling that they have learned something that will help the student get more from his school experience. Sincerity, understanding, and positive regard are as appropriate in parent conferences as they are in other interpersonal relationships and will help ensure the two-way communication which is necessary for good parent conferences. A pamphlet written for high school teachers states that:

> The parent must feel that he can express his real thoughts and feelings with the knowledge that he will be understood by a sympathetic person who is as interested in and concerned as he about the subject of their conversation. . . . It is very important for the teacher to find out how the parent is actually thinking and feeling about his child. The teacher cannot understand or interpret the child's behavior with any accuracy until he knows the parent attitudes.[1]

Remember the Student   The subject of parent conferences ought not to be forgotten. If you can remember when your parents talked to your teachers about you, you can sympathize with the student. He wants to know what is going on. He may also be resentful. He doesn't want everyone knowing his business and talking about him.

> The adolescent, in gradually gaining independence, needs some privacy of thought and action, some freedom to explore and assert himself which will not be known by his parents. The adolescent may liken a parent-teacher conference to a conspiracy to deprive him of privacy or freedom. Parents and teachers alike will not be successful in their purposes for conferring until the youngster realizes that his dignity, individuality, and pride will not be violated, and that the discussion is for his benefit.[2]

One way to assure the student that his dignity and individuality are not being violated is to be as open as possible. In most

[1] *With Parents Like That*, Guidance Series for Teachers No. 5 (Harrisburg, Penn.: Department of Public Instruction, Commonwealth of Pennsylvania, 1961), pp. 29–30.

[2] Walter F. Johnson, Buford Stefflre, and Roy A. Edelfelt, *Pupil Personnel and Guidance Services* (New York, McGraw-Hill Book Company, 1961), p. 68.

cases, he should know when and why a conference is being held. Occasionally, a teacher's best judgment will be that he should talk to the parents without the student's knowledge. On the whole, however, it is best to include the student as much as possible. It is his life and he is old enough to be taking responsibility for it. He may be asked to set up the appointment or actually be included in the conferences. Three-way conferences can be very successful, if it is clear that the purpose of the conference is to help, not accuse, the student. In this type of conference there can be no misunderstanding about what the teacher tells his parents about him and vice-versa; he can give his side of the picture directly and his opinion of any suggestions made.

EXAMPLES

1. Mrs. Hallowell is talking with Joyce's science teacher, Mrs. Carpenter.

> *Mrs. Hallowell:*   I know Joyce isn't a very good student but I'm sure she could do better than she is. She does her homework because I make sure of that but she has a hard time understanding some of it.

> *Mrs. Carpenter:*   Yes, she's done her homework regularly. You can see here in the rollbook that it's all checked off, but you can also see from these papers here that sometimes she does it pretty carelessly. Does she spend much time on it?

> *Mrs. Hallowell:*   Well, she loves to get together with her friends. She's good about doing her homework first but I suppose she hurries it to get it over with.

> *Mrs. Carpenter:*   Her friends are pretty important to her?

> *Mrs. Hallowell:*   Yes, and I can't blame her too much because she has had a hard time making friends since we moved. Now she has several good friends but they aren't very interested in school either. Do you think I should be stricter with her and make her put more time on her homework? Sometimes I just don't know what is best. School is so important these days and I just can't get her to realize it.

> *Mrs. Carpenter:*   You know Joyce better than I do. I can't tell you what is best. I do know that she is having

a hard time in science. She does need to do better if she is going to pass. Some of her work is pretty good so I think she can pass if we help her. Do you have any ideas of how I could help?

Mrs. Hallowell: You know, I think she really doesn't understand some of it. If you could explain it to her so she wouldn't feel so stupid, it might help. She tells me she hates science because she just can't get it.

Mrs. Carpenter has already learned some things about Joyce that may help her: that her mother is genuinely concerned, that Joyce has trouble making friends, that she has difficulty understanding science. Mrs. Hallowell is confirmed in her knowledge that Joyce is doing poorly, has learned that Joyce occasionally does good work, and is beginning to believe that Mrs. Carpenter is really interested in Joyce. Mrs. Carpenter has resisted giving advice to Mrs. Hallowell though she may do so later in making appropriate suggestions about study habits or other matters on which she has information. She has encouraged Mrs. Hallowell to talk by listening and trying to understand, and by so doing she has learned more of use to her than had she buried her with a flood of information about Joyce's shortcomings. She has been honest and straightforward. This conference exhibits to some extent many of the desired qualities in good counseling. Mrs. Hallowell's last comment suggests that she is beginning to trust Mrs. Carpenter enough to tell her things that she did not tell her at first.

2.   Ricky is too much. Mrs. Schwartz is an experienced teacher but she finds that Ricky tries her patience more than any student she has had in Spanish for several years. His behavior shows an ingenuity and cleverness not duplicated in his work, which is only passable. Mrs. Schwartz has asked Ricky's mother to come see her together with Ricky.

Mrs. Schwartz: I wonder if between the three of us we can work out something so that Ricky and I can get along better. I've sent him out of the room twice in the last week. He disrupts the entire class by coming in late, by talking out in the middle of class, and by starting other boys in the class laughing. Yesterday, Ricky, when I asked you to sit down, you said you would in a moment. That was after the bell had rung.

Mother: I knew his grades weren't so good but I didn't realize he was acting up in class so much. His father can take care of that.

Mrs. Schwartz: Well, I wasn't thinking of that so much. I thought maybe we could get at what makes you act up so much, Ricky, so that you could settle down more. Can you help us any?

Ricky: Nah.

Mother: Why can't you behave, Ricky?

Ricky: I'm not the only one.

Mrs. Schwartz: You're right about that, Ricky, but I think you're the leader. Is that right?

Ricky: Maybe.

Mrs. Schwartz: I guess it seems as if your mother and I were sort of ganging up on you, but this really is your chance to tell us your side of it. If I could understand, I might be able to make Spanish better for you.

Ricky: You couldn't ever make Spanish better for me. I hate it. Most classes are dull but this is the worst. Who needs it?

Mrs. Schwartz: Well, if you dislike a subject it *is* hard to pay attention to class. I've felt that way myself sometimes when I was in school.

After a shaky start, this conference is at the point where progress might be made. Mrs. Schwartz began by putting Ricky on the spot with his mother. When she realized what she had done—and she need not necessarily have foreseen the mother's response—she tried to retrieve the situation by pulling Ricky into the conference more rather than talking about him. Not unnaturally, he was suspicious at first. With many students it would take even longer before they would believe that this adult authority figure, the teacher, really wants to know what he thinks. This suspicion is hardly surprising, as schools in general rarely solicit student opinion and when they do tend to ignore it. So Ricky does not respond easily to Mrs. Schwartz. Fortunately, when he does respond with his feeling about Spanish, she is able to accept his feeling, to understand it, and not discourse on the need for Spanish. This is the beginning of understanding between them. Next she will need to pull the mother back into the conference so three-way understanding can be reached.

ROLE-PLAYING SITUATION

Because three-way conferences are relatively unused but also have such good possibilities, we are suggesting a role-playing situation which includes teacher, parent and student. After trying this one, you may want to vary it by redoing it without the student to see what difference it makes. You may also want to devise completely different situations out of your own experience.

Here is some information about each participant. You will have to decide the kind of school it takes place in and build up more information about each person.

> *Mike*, a ninth-grader, is not doing well in English. Although he has been doing his homework, he is behind with his book reports and has refused to do one assignment which required that he write a poem. He likes school better than he ever has before, especially its social aspects. For the first time, he is passing all his subjects but by a narrow margin. English is the worst subject for him. He prefers television to reading.

> *Mr. Howland* is a second-year teacher dedicated to getting ninth-graders settled down and working hard on what he believes is a subject essential to their future success. He likes his students, spends long hours preparing and grading, encourages discussion in the classroom, and sets high standards. Judging from Mike's homework, and occasional good papers, he believes that Mike could do better work. It disturbs him that Mike never contributes to class discussion.

> *Mrs. Parmelee* and her husband have spent long hours worrying about Mike's school work. He is their oldest boy. His sister, a senior, is a good student. Mrs. Parmelee has encouraged Mike to work harder, checks on his homework, but never punishes him in any way for his poor report cards. She is especially worried now because she feels that high school grades are more important than those thus far. It is she who asked for the conference.

Before you role play, discuss the goals of a conference like this. What should Mr. Howland hope for and how can he best accomplish it? What does Mrs. Parmelee hope for? What do you think Mike expects? After role playing, you will want to discuss what has been accomplished. How good was the communication? How do you know? How could it have been improved? What feelings were involved? Did Mr. Howland listen?

SUMMARY

Open communication between parents and teachers enhances teaching effectiveness. Such communication is often blocked by suspicion and fear on both sides. If teachers understand how parents view them and the school, they are more easily able to open up communication. It is especially important for teachers in ghetto schools to understand parental attitudes toward school and to take the initiative in establishing some lines of communication.

Communication between parents and teachers should be two-way. Good parent conferences are ones in which both parties feel they have learned something that will help the student get more from his school experience.

SUGGESTED READINGS

Bailard, Virginia, and Ruth Strang, *Parent-Teacher Conferences*. New York: McGraw-Hill Book Company, 1964. One of the few books directed to parent conferences. Written for teachers at all levels, but high school teachers will find it helpful.

Hymes, James L., Jr., *Effective Home-School Relations*. Englewood Cliffs, N.J.: Prentice-Hall, 1953. Written mostly for elementary school teachers, the general discussion about the need for home-school relations is good as well as the section about high schools on pp. 219–24.

Nordberg, H. Orville, James M. Bradfield, and William C. Odell, *Secondary School Teaching*. New York: The Macmillan Company, 1962. A sound discussion on working with parents and the community in Chapter 17. Other texts on secondary teaching will have similar chapters.

9

When Things Get Difficult

Academic counseling, educational-vocational counseling, parent conferences—these all fall easily under a teacher's responsibilities and competencies. The trouble is that although we have made neat categories thus far, real-life students and parents have a way of moving out of these categories into areas which teachers may feel they would rather not discuss. Ricky's mother may in the next sentence be telling how mean her husband is when he drinks. Debbie, having found Mr. Schreiner an understanding person with whom to talk about her future, may soon be confiding in him about boyfriend troubles. Sometimes teachers feel that they must refer students who present more of a problem than they feel they can work with, but teachers can at other times counsel effectively with such students. Moreover, they do not always have someone to whom they can refer. Therefore, let us look at some of the things to consider in talking with students about what are called personal or non-school problems—those which seem to be not directly related to school, though by their effect on total behavior are indeed closely

131

related to school—and then let us look at ways and problems of referring students for further help.

Listening

That listening is of paramount importance in all counseling— and interpersonal relationships—has been stated again and again as we have discussed various approaches to counseling and various situations encountered by teachers. To understand means listening. To empathize means listening. Listening shows respect, concern, and care. But how hard it is to do! We are bombarded by so much to which to listen throughout each day that we become adept at ignoring what we do not want to hear. Indeed we must do so in order to maintain our sanity. When a student is talking with us, however, we must learn to listen.

Real listening is hard work. It takes intense concentration, especially if we are listening both to the words and to what is behind them. To listen to someone who is trying to tell of his problems and concerns means that we must cut out everything else so that there is nothing but the two of us. If we are wondering what to say next, we are not listening. All our energy must be devoted to what he is saying. If we want to test how well we are listening, then our responses may be ones such as,

> Are you saying that . . .
>
> You mean that . . .
>
> It seems to you that . . .

If he says, "Yeah, that's it," then we feel a real glow of satisfaction that we have understood what he was saying. If he says, "No, that's not what I mean," then we ask him to explain it a little more and are glad that he trusted us enough to respond honestly.

In order to improve your listening abilities, we suggest that you practice by listening in ordinary conversation to what those around you are saying.

Accepting Unpleasant Feelings

When we hear someone express an unpleasant feeling such as hatred, anger, or discouragement, our usual reaction is to pretend not to have heard it or to tell the other person that it really isn't as bad as he thinks. We do not like to hear unpleasant things or believe that people are as unhappy or as angry as they say. Middle-class culture frowns on direct expressions of emotions, especially unhappy ones.

In a classroom role-playing situation, the student said to the counselor, "I really *hate* my brother." The counselor gasped out. "Oh, No!" He could not believe that anyone could say such a thing and started out to convince the student that she did not really mean it. In later discussion, the role-playing student said she did not think the counselor could help her because he could not understand her feelings.

If people are unhappy, if they do have unpleasant feelings, they need to be able to talk about them. If a student really does hate his father, it will do him no good to keep this feeling bottled up inside of him. If he can talk it out with someone who will listen and accept his feelings he can come to understand his own feelings better and learn to handle them. Feelings of hostility, anger, hate, or bitterness must be allowed to come to the top where they can be looked at and understood before they can be dissipated and replaced by more positive feelings. It is important, therefore, for anyone who wants to work with the personal concerns of students to be able to accept unpleasant feelings, and to try to understand how students with these feelings see their situation. If we can understand how a student's world looks to him, we can come closer to understanding why he feels the way he does. This, of course, is empathy.

Many students live in unbelievably difficult circumstances. As we listen to them, our wonder is that they are able to get along as well as they do. Here, teachers have another temptation to avoid. Not unnaturally, they are sympathetic. Sympathy is a laudable emotion but not always helpful to the recipient. It will not help him to feel sorry for himself. A teacher can help a student in a bad situation by showing understanding, respect, and faith that he can cope with the situation with which he has to live. To avoid oversympathizing and to encourage the student to recognize and find his own strength with which to meet the situation takes skill and courage on the part of the teacher or counselor. So often, teachers want to move in and change the situation for the student. Some situations, certainly those within the school, can be changed, but more often these students of whom we are speaking are in situations over which the school has no control: poverty, alcoholic parents, serious illness, personal tragedies or losses. Both teachers and students have to learn to live with these situations and cope with them intelligently. Listening to and accepting unpleasant feelings does not mean excusing the student from that which must be done. He needs to be heard but also helped to plan constructively for the future.

We suggest that you stop here and think about how you would respond to statements like those which follow. What could you say which would show your desire to understand?

Student: I really hate my brother.

Student: I'm too stupid to ever learn anything.

Parent: My husband's fine when he's sober but when he's drunk, he's mean. He beats the kids.

Parent: My wife is dying. The children know it now.

Student: My pop left us a year ago. Mom works and I'm supposed to do all the housework and take care of the kids.

Student: I hate school and everyone here hates me. I'm the wrong color.

Student: This school was OK until they started bussing Negroes to it. I hate them and I'll make it as hard for them as I can.

Student: I can't stand Mrs. Mallory. She's a terrible teacher.

Parent: Joe's a lazy no-good. He's not even mine. We took him in when my sister-in-law died.

Don't Pry

It helps students who have unpleasant feelings to be able to talk about them, but not before they are ready to. Some feelings are so frightening to a person that he cannot recognize them. To force him to do so prematurely could be very damaging. A good way to avoid getting in over one's head in talking with a student is not to probe or pry. Avoid questions such as, "Why do you hate your sister?" "How do you feel about your father?" There are lots of things one might like to know in order to satisfy curiosity, but satisfying curiosity is not the purpose of conferences with students or parents. It helps to know some things in order to understand a student's behavior, but most important is trying to understand how he feels. Most teachers do not have the background to diagnose a student's problems. However, most certainly have the human capacity to convey understanding and concern to students, to be interested in them, and to really listen to what they say. Asking probing questions is both unnecessary and dangerous.

Sex, Values, Drugs, and Beliefs

Adolescents are engaged in developing their values and beliefs. Some of them have values pushed at them by home, school, and church. Others are left on their own. Some are rebelling against adult values. Others are searching for values they can hold onto. They question some of the religious ideas with which they have been brought up. They wonder how far to go in their dating. They see their friends cheating in school. Some are experimenting with drugs and tempting others to join. They are faced with questions of war and peace. They need and want to talk over these kinds of things with trusted adults as well as with their friends.

Boy and Pine discuss the adolescent's need to work out for *himself* a personal code of conduct and point out that:

> A society of conflicting values does not make the formation of a personal code of values an easy task for the typical adolescent, who is usually highly idealistic. The values of the home, the church, the school, the community, the adolescent peer group, the various subcultures of society, and the mass media do not jibe with each other; in fact, often they are diametrically opposed. . . . Adults administer and interpret the culture in moral terms, but when the adolescent applies these terms to the conduct of parents and other adults he all too often finds the ideal lacking. . . . One type of behavior is rewarded by one's peers; the opposite type, by parents and adults. Even within his nature, the adolescent finds conflict between his highly idealistic values and his need to be part of the group and hold (at least on the surface) to the group values even though they may contradict his own. The establishment of a personal set of values amid many con-

flicting standards can be achieved through a counseling relationship that permits the adolescent to *be*.[1]

Kemp writes,

It is essential that counselors be open to the existential quest of their students. Many counselors assume that the high school student is interested only in those goals that provide security and status. Perhaps he does not recognize a deeper hunger in the counselee for fear of acknowledging emptiness within himself.[2]

Too often, adolescents cannot find adults who will listen to their questions and doubts and help them think their way through to at least temporary answers. Many adults, among them teachers, are likely to give answers instead of listening, to try to convince these adolescents that adult values are right without trying to understand their doubts and questions. Teachers too have doubts and questions which are hard to face. When we have unresolved doubts which we do not acknowledge, we find it hard to listen to a student who raises the same doubts and increases our own anxiety. We do not have all the answers to the perplexing problems of our age and do not always have enough security to share our own perplexities with our students. Part of good counseling entails openness on the part of the counselor. If a teacher is able to say, "I'm not sure either," he is on the way to open communication with the student. In the framework of open communication, the student can find some easing of his doubts and anxieties and is then freed to begin to work out his own values.

Another reason that teachers sometimes do not listen to students with these kinds of concerns is fear that they will become engaged in a controversial subject which they feel ought not be discussed in the public schools, for example, sex or religion. However, schools are educational institutions where students should be able to ask questions, express doubts, and discuss beliefs. Teachers should not indoctrinate or convince students of the rightness of particular beliefs but they can certainly listen and respond in ways which will help students extend their thinking. Where students need particular information about sex, teachers can refer them to school nurse teachers or family physicians who are equipped to give accurate information. On questions of reli-

[1] Angelo V. Boy and Gerald J. Pine, *The School Counselor: A Reconceptualization* Boston: Houghton Mifflin Company, 1968), pp. 80–81.

[2] C. Gratton Kemp, *Intangibles in Counseling* (Boston: Houghton Mifflin Company, 1967), p. 115.

gion, they can refer students to their own minister, priest, or rabbi.

Conflicts in Values   Counselors, believing that each person has the right to make his own decisions, must decide whether or not they extend this belief to giving each person the right to choose his own values even though they are in conflict with those of the counselor or those of society, or even injurious to the well-being of the person. They have approached this problem in several different ways. One approach is to say that they accept the counselee as a person but do not accept values that lead to unacceptable behavior such as cheating. Other counselors say that one cannot accept a person apart from his values and therefore must be open to values and behaviors very different from his own.[3] Recently, some writers in the field of counseling and psychotherapy have been saying that counselors and therapists have erred badly in not taking a more active role in responding to moral issues presented by counselees. They question the traditionally neutral stance of therapists.[4]

Taking students and their value concerns seriously is important. Whatever is serious to them is serious to us. Too often, adults make light either of adolescent concerns with the thought they will grow out of them, or of adolescent views of current social and political problems with the thought that they are "too young to understand." In so doing, adults underestimate both the seriousness of the concerns and the potential maturity with which adolescents approach vital concerns. Given a teacher or counselor who listens with respect, they show remarkable insight and understanding.

A physical education teacher was listening to a student talk about the differences between adolescent and adult perceptions of the use of drugs.

Teacher: Most older people just don't understand these things that kids are interested in now, is that it?

[3]Dugald S. Arbuckle, *Counseling: Philosophy, Theory and Practice* (Boston: Allyn & Bacon, Inc., 1965), Chapter VIII.
[4]Perry London, *The Modes and Morals of Psychotherapy* (New York: Holt, Rinehart & Winston, Inc., 1964). William Glasser, *Reality Therapy* (New York: Harper & Row, Publishers, 1965). O. H. Mowrer, "Science, Sex, and Values," *Personnel and Guidance Journal*, Vol. 42, No. 8 (April, 1964), 746–52. Edmund G. Williamson, "The Counselor as Technique," *Personnel and Guidance Journal*, Vol. 41, No. 2 (October, 1962), 108–11.

Student: I don't know, I think a lot of it is having to do with set things. You know, you have social mores that have been established and things that are done and not done, and I was watching this TV panel last night for parents. They were discussing what kids are doing now and these parents were mostly people with children in high school or college. It is a very hard thing to get over the hurdle of setting up something new, a new establishment in society. They had liquor and liquor was the accepted high. And they see nothing wrong with liquor.

Teacher: Older people seem to get more rigid in their ideas of the things they are willing to accept?

Student: Understandably so. It's not anything. I mean I don't hold it against adults that find it hard to accept things or take longer. They've grown up in their set ways. Things have not changed that much for them or things that they were born with are still that way—some of the things. The things that have changed gradually, they can accept, but these new types of revolutions are something that came so late in a lot of their lives that it's something really, you know, really hard to accept.

Whether or not one agrees with the views of this student, one can hardly fault the sincerity, thoughtfulness, and maturity of her statements. This kind of maturity is duplicated frequently when teachers take the time to take students seriously.

We have said before that counselors, and hence teachers when they are counseling, must learn to be sensitive to and acceptant of values different from their own. They cannot listen to and accept the many different kinds of students who come to them for help and/or teaching unless they are able to understand and accept the many different backgrounds from which the students come. They must learn that what is and has been right for them may not be right for someone else, and make every effort to see the world from other people's perspectives. On the other hand, a neutral stance on questions of values, morals, and behavior is difficult for teachers (and many counselors) to achieve. They believe that education is important, cheating wrong (even though graduate students in schools of education have been known to cheat), and disciplined behavior necessary. Students know that schools and hence teachers generally stand for values such as these. If these values are indeed important to teachers, they are less than honest or congruent if they pretend otherwise. We would conclude that teachers when they are counseling cannot help but let their values show. If it is true that a counselee's person and values cannot be separated, then the same thing holds true for the teacher or counselor, and if this be so, how do teachers and counselors behave when students raise value concerns?

At the time a teacher is counseling with an individual, his responsibility is to the individual, although the individual must always be considered within the context of society. His concern is to understand the world of students, help him think through his concerns and understand the consequences of his behavior, accept his confusion and perplexity, and listen to what he has to say. If the teacher feels that it is appropriate for him to make his own values clear, then he can do so, for in so doing he is being open and sincere. If he does not do so, then the student is left to guess what his reactions are or to suspect that he is not being honest. If a teacher feels that cheating is wrong he can say so and explain why. He can at the same time listen in order to understand why the student has cheated and help him understand too, why he has cheated and what the consequences may be. He can remain concerned with the student and interested in him even if he does not approve of parts of his behavior or beliefs. He can also refrain from preaching or moralizing, neither of which are appropriate in counseling because they contribute to dependency rather than to increased maturity and understanding. If the relationship between student and teacher is strong enough, the kind of relationship which was described as a counseling relationship, then it can stand and even benefit from counselor disclosure of values. His values are already implicit in his behavior, as observed by the student. A student chooses to talk with a particular teacher because there is already the beginning of a counseling relationship between them, developed by classroom interchanges and after-school chats. He often is asking for the honest opinion of the teacher and is entitled to receive it.

The danger of destroying the relationship lies in responses which say to the student, "If you keep on behaving like this I will not like you," or "Anyone who thinks the way you do is no good." The important thing is to continue to care, even though there are wide differences in the way teacher and student look at the situation or concern under discussion.

Referring Students

When teachers encounter students with problems of such dimension that they feel the students need more help than they can give, they refer these students for more specialized help. School counselors, too, refer students who need more specialized help than they can give. Referring students well requires good judgment and knowledge of referral sources.

In schools where there are well organized guidance and pupil personnel services, teachers refer students to the guidance office, which is then responsible for any further referrals. Some schools have many services but leave the teachers to decide to which specialist to refer students. In either case, teachers refer students only to school services. Referral to community agencies is outside a teacher's responsibilities unless such responsibility has been clearly given to him by school authorities. Gibson and Higgins see the teacher as playing an important role in the referral process, ". . . a key person in identifying pupils with counseling needs, preparing them for referral, and actually referring them to the school counselor."[5]

When To Refer   When to refer depends upon the teacher, the student, and the available resources. Teachers usually realize when a student's concerns may be too deep or extensive for them to work with: the student who worries about homosexuality, the boy whose parents are getting a divorce, the girl who is pregnant, the student who has no friends and is so unresponsive that he hardly seems to be in class. Each such case, however, would have to be carefully considered, preferably with the help of the school counselor. What if the teacher appears to be the only one who has been able to establish a relationship with the student? What if there are no referral resources? Not all schools have school counselors, not all communities have mental health clinics at hand. The teacher may know that he is not the one to counsel with a student who is disturbed, but if there is no one else to whom the student can go, what then? Time after time the question of referral comes down to a matter of the individual judgment of the teacher as he balances his own competence and

[5]Robert L. Gibson and Robert E. Higgins, *Techniques of Guidance: An Approach to Pupil Analysis* (Chicago: Science Research Associates, Inc., 1966), p. 30.

time against the needs of the student and the resources of the community.

Many teachers seem to fear that they will go in over their heads in counseling—that blundering in too far and, too fast, they will hurt students. Teachers are unlikely to hurt students whom they are genuinely interested and whom they are sincerely trying to help. Students respond to the concern the teacher shows for them more than to his skills as a counselor. They will forgive many mistakes if they believe teachers are trying to help them. A psychiatrist, making the point that teachers should not deal with disturbed children, was faced with the fact that teachers do, in fact, deal with disturbed students day in and day out because they have them in class day in and day out. He finally said that teachers were unlikely to harm these children if they were really trying to help.

A former student describes, far better than we can, how teachers can help even if all they do is listen. When Lucille was in high school, she was miserably unhappy. She had several episodes manifesting serious problems. There were no psychological or referral sources available, not even a trained counselor. One of the authors worked closely with Lucille over a period of a year or two. At one time she told Lucille she couldn't help her, feeling that Lucille needed more help than she could give her. Lucille eventually spent some time under treatment in the state hospital. Since then, as a happily married wife and mother, she has corresponded with the author. One time the author wrote to ask her opinion about how teachers could help students. Following are the questions and Lucille's answers to them.

What do you think teachers should know so that they can help students more?

Lucille: I feel I do know some things that teachers don't take time for because the classes are too full and that is, make all, and I do say make all, kids feel they are wanted and most of all needed. Let me explain. A person that is unhappy at home does not find the love they so need, the understanding some parents don't take time to give. Well, they, of course, look for it elsewhere, in the classroom.

Do you think someone could have helped you sooner?

Lucille: Yes! Let me explain. My life of growing up was hard. I was one of these persons that didn't feel wanted or needed or even loved. My home life was always put to these words, "If it weren't for you, we could of had," etc. So, at school when a *teacher* or *you* or the *school nurse* would talk to me, I felt someone cared.

You see I feel that a teacher is more or less of a second mother. She should let the class know that if they want someone to talk to they would be glad to. I was not an "A" student but I was not dumb either, but I can tell you this, not one of my teachers, besides you, the school nurse, and Miss B., made me feel that I could talk to them. Oh, don't get me wrong, they were nice, but that was all. You know yourself there are many such as me, and if a person can't get love and understanding at home or at school, what does one do? Why, now why, do you think I looked for love in the only three people in high school that made and gave me reason to want to live. Yes, I know why I was sick, just hope you can better understand. I'm sorry for a lot of things that happened then; one being—when I was told by my parents they were going to send me away, I again looked for help, that being in you. Yes, always I was afraid of my father and many times you of all people I told. But, the one day my world fell from me was when I was talking to you and your words were as I have never forgotten, "Lucille, I can't help you." Well, to you it was just words but to me you were saying I don't care what happens to you. That was when I wanted to die and so the State Hospital came into my life. In all this I've been trying to say never give up. *Never say to anyone, "I can't help," because you can, just try to have them, the person to whom you are talking to talk things over, let them get it out, let them know you care what happens to them. Never say you can't help because if you do, their world is gone, and, once this happens, they won't care.* (Italics are the authors'.)

How To Refer   Lucille tells us how much a teacher's interest can mean to a student. A teacher, taking the time to listen, helped make it possible for Lucille to stay in school as long as she did. Lucille also tells us how hard it is to make a referral. The person whom she trusted told her she could not help her. That person was only trying to say that Lucille needed more help than she could give her. Untrained then as a counselor, she felt she was not the one who could help Lucille. To Lucille, this was rejection by the one person she trusted.

The cardinal rule in referral is to do it in such a way that the student will not feel you are rejecting him. The student has found someone to whom he can talk. Referral ought not to mean that the student can no longer talk with the teacher who is his friend nor be helped by him. It ought to mean that another door has opened up. The teacher needs to make the student feel that he will continue to be interested in him, that he can still be available, even though he is suggesting that someone else might help the student further.

When a teacher considers a referral, his own feelings enter into how he approaches it. In this day and age, referrals for counseling or psychological help are often seen as a common aspect of normal development—at least for other people. But going for help in solving one's problems may be something we ourselves would be loath or even ashamed to do. If so, we approach referring someone else for help with reluctance, projecting our feelings to him so that we think he will be shocked, alarmed, or insulted if we suggest that he see his counselor. What must be remembered is that when a person talks with a teacher about a severe problem, he is asking for help. If he didn't want help, he wouldn't be talking with the teacher. He has already taken the first step and has perhaps already considered going to a counselor or a psychologist. Rather than see a referral as it would look to himself, the teacher must try to see it as it looks to the student. Part of the process of referring is to explore the student's readiness for it, to try to get some idea of how he would respond to referral before actually making the suggestion. It might be apparent that the student was just waiting for someone to give him a little push in the direction of the counselor; on the other hand, it might be apparent that the student would immediately reject the prospect of referral. In the latter case, the teacher may need to talk with him two or three times in order to help him accept referral.

If a student rejects referral, the teacher can accept this rejection for the present and keep the door open. Maintaining a friendly and interested relationship with the student is helping him even if the teacher is sure he needs different, more intensive help. Later on the student may be able to accept referral. In the meantime, he has someone who can at least listen to him.

Sometimes a student who rejects referral presents such a difficult problem that the teacher feels he must share the responsibility with someone else. The student may need more time than the teacher can give him. He may seem close to action which would endanger himself or someone else. He may be causing more trouble in class than the teacher can tolerate. In cases like these, the teacher should always feel free to discuss the situation with the school counselor or other responsible school official. Preferably, he should ask the student first for permission to discuss his problem with the counselor. If this does not seem possible, he should be able to talk with the counselor as a professional colleague without betraying the trust of the student who has come to him. Together, the teacher and the counselor can decide on a tentative course of action. The teacher may continue seeing the student occasionally, while conferring with the counselor about the best way to talk with the student. The teacher may ask the student if he would mind if the counselor called him in. In some cases, it might be necessary for the teacher to tell the student that he felt he had to refer him to the counselor. Whenever a teacher is in doubt about whether or not to refer a student, he can consult with the counselor.

EXAMPLES

1.   Fred is talking with one of his teachers after school.

Miss Jones: Your parents just don't like your friends, is that it?

Fred: Yes, they think they're a bad influence on me.

Miss Jones: Are they?

Fred: I don't think so. We get in some trouble now and then, nothing much, but the police are always picking on us. They don't like it when we stand around the store and talk. We're not doing nothin' but talking, but they park and watch us.

Miss Jones: They seem sort of suspicious of you all?

Fred: Yeah, they don't like the kids that dress the way we do. My parents don't either. I can't do anything right, even when I try.

Miss Jones: John, are you saying that you don't like the way things are going right now?

Fred: Not really. But I worry. I don't ever stay around the house anymore. I can't talk with my parents.

Miss Jones: Would you like to be able to talk things over with them?

Fred: I dunno. I guess so. I'm really sort of confused. I mean I'm not sure what I want, what I can be.

Miss Jones: I guess the fact you're talking with me now means you'd like to be talking some of this over with someone. I'm glad to talk with you, but I wonder if you'd thought of talking with your counselor. He's used to talking to kids with problems like yours.

Fred: Nah, he's just for school problems and he doesn't like kids like me either. I don't like school much.

Miss Jones: I think you'd find he'd listen to you and be able to help you work out some of your ideas, maybe help you get some idea of what direction you want to take. You do want to talk with someone and that's what he's there for.

Fred: Well, I like talking with you because you know me, but I know you've got a lot of other things to do.

Miss Jones: It isn't that, well, in part I guess it is. I have to teach all my classes and give extra help to students who need it. I don't have as much time as the counselor to talk with individual students, much as I like it. I like talking with you and, if you see your counselor, I'd still be talking with you, I hope, but the counselor could really give you more time in working things out. Why don't you give it a try?

Fred: Well, maybe.

Miss Jones: O.K., stop back tomorrow and let me know what you decide.

Miss Jones has recognized that the student has a lot on his mind. She knows that students like that often drift into trouble. Fred seems to realize this too and is asking for help. Miss Jones suggests the school counselor but leaves the door open for the student to continue talking with her.

2. This morning the students had an assembly on narcotics presented by the local police department. Mr. Macdougall followed up the assembly with a discussion in his social studies class. This afternoon, Frank stops in after school.

Frank: You know, Mr. Macdougall, that assembly on drugs, it has me sort of worried, especially after the discussion in class.

Mr. Macdougall: What is it that worried you, Frank?

Frank: I really don't know what's right.

Mr. Macdougall: Right about what?

Frank: Well, I don't know. It's just that . . . I don't know.

[Mr. Macdougall waits while Frank thinks.]

Frank: Well, it's that I'm not interested in drugs myself but some of my friends are. They've been having parties and invited me. I think it's wrong or maybe I'm just scared. They're getting mad at me because I won't go along with them.

Mr. Macdougall: You're pretty sure drugs are wrong yourself but your friends sort of make you wonder, is that it?

Frank: Yeah, I don't want to be different but so many kids are smoking marijuana I think maybe it must be all right.

Mr. Macdougall: Sometimes you're not so sure it's wrong.

Mr. Macdougall is trying hard to let Frank express his doubts so that he can think honestly about his feelings about narcotics. He is not rushing him. Some of you may think that Mr. Macdougall should point out the dangers of narcotics but Frank has already heard all that. Now he has to think things out for himself. Mr. Macdougall may well be uneasy in this situation but he thinks it is important for Frank to be able to talk with a trusted adult about something as important as this.

ROLE-PLAYING SITUATIONS

1.   Kathy is a 16-year-old junior in high school, an average student, moderately attractive, friendly and responsible. Miss Engelhard has seen her several times in the hall and at lunch with a boy from a racially different background. Today, she is in Miss Engelhard's room after school chatting about this and

that but giving the impression that there is something she really wants to talk about. When Miss Engelhard conveys this impression to her, she says:

> Oh, yes! There is something I want to talk about. I don't know how to begin, I mean, I don't know how you feel about it. The trouble is, you know, I'm going with a boy. And he's a (Gentile, Jew, Negro, Puerto Rican, Mexican). Mother says I shouldn't go with him, that it will only lead to trouble, but I don't see why. He's fun, and he's nice to be with. He's one of the nicest boys I've ever met. Some of my friends say they'll drop me if I keep going with him. I don't know *what* to think!

Before role playing, talk about the values, beliefs, and feelings which govern how Miss Engelhard will respond to Kathy. How will her own feelings affect her responses? Discuss the confusion which Kathy feels as she tries to find her way to her own values and beliefs. Would a referral be appropriate?

2.   Mike is talking with Mr. Cohen after school in the parking lot. Mr. Cohen has congratulated Mike on his election to National Honor Society. He notices that Mike does not seem very pleased.

> *Mr. Cohen*:   What's the matter, Mike? Aren't you proud of yourself?
>
> *Mike*:   Not really. Half the kids that get in get there by cheating.

In role playing the situation from here, how should Mr. Cohen respond? How are his personal values going to affect the way he responds? Should he try to get Mike to give him the names of people who have cheated? Is it possible that Mike is trying to tell Mr. Cohen something more—that he, Mike, has cheated, is not sure how he feels about it, and wants to talk with a trusted adult?

3.   A social studies teacher has been teaching about the period of the Protestant Reformation. During some discussion concerning the charges and countercharges made during that period by the reformers and by the Pope, he noted that Penny looked particularly interested though she did not take part. Later, she

comes in to see him. She wants to talk with him about some of the things said in class. With a Roman Catholic father, and a Protestant mother, she is being brought up as a Roman Catholic. She is beginning to doubt some of the things she has been taught. She can't talk about these doubts at home.

Can the teacher counsel with Penny? Are there some dangers involved? If he turns her off, to whom can she go? Many adolescents question what they have been told all their lives not only about religion but about the moral standards accepted, at least verbally, by most adults. Can teachers help their students by letting them discuss their doubts or is it better for them to allow no questioning of adult standards?

4.   Instead of role playing a situation already set up for you, try to devise one of your own. Someone in the group must know of a situation where values were involved. Let this person describe the situation, then decide upon the role players. If there are more than two people in the role-playing group, let several people try counseling to see if some find more effective ways than others. The best judge of the effectiveness of the counseling is the person playing the role of the student.

SUMMARY

Teachers have many occasions on which to counsel or talk with students and parents. Some conferences are initiated by teachers, others by students or parents. The occasion may center around academic problems, educational-vocational planning, or personal concerns. Whatever the focus of the conference, the teacher who counsels tries to understand the world of the student, listen to what he has to say, and help him work out his concerns. He does not give him answers, persuade him toward any particular course of action, or preach. He tries to accord to each student the respect and dignity which all people are owed. In parent conferences, teachers strive for two-way communication so that they can work together in helping students.

Adolescents want to find adults whom they trust, who will listen to them, and who will help them. The autobiography of an eleventh-grade boy expresses this need well. He describes the way in which he lost confidence in himself through certain early school experiences, encountered one guidance counselor who did not seem to care, and then another who wanted to help. The second guidance counselor helped him choose a course of study which he has enjoyed and in which he has found success. In conclusion he writes:

> I like life and want to go on living for a long time. I have certain theories, ideas, wants, and needs that I must explore and find out for myself. I need help and want help but I just can't go to anyone and say, "I want help." I wish that a mass of genuine humanitarians would come from Mars and become the teachers and counselors because one mistake when you are young can lead to a wasted life.

Students should not have to wait for an invasion from Mars to find human people with whom they can talk but should be able to find teachers who will recognize their need for help. Teachers who respond intelligently and thoughtfully to individual students will find their teaching enriched and their understanding of adolescents constantly broadened.

Sometimes teachers encounter situations, either with students or parents, which they find difficult to handle. Listening, accepting unpleasant feelings, and resisting the temptation to ask probing questions can help teachers handle these situations. When teachers question whether or not they can handle a situation, they can consult with a school counselor or other responsible school official. In many cases, they will want to refer students or parents for further help. When referral is necessary, it is important for the teacher to make it easy for those referred to feel they can return to him if they want to; he must not give the impression that he is rejecting them.

Adolescents are looking for help in formulating their values and beliefs about themselves, others, and the world in which they live. Students often turn to teachers for this help. It is important for teachers not to be afraid to counsel with their students about values and beliefs.

Earlier in the chapter, a student named Lucille wrote a letter about how teachers can help students. What she wrote at the end is worth repeating and remembering:

> Never say to anyone "I can't help," because you can, just try to have them, the person to whom you are talking, to talk things over, let them get it out, let them know you

care what happens to them. Never say you can't help because if you do, their world is gone, and once this happens, they won't care.

SUGGESTED READINGS

American Association for Health, Physical Education and Recreation, *Drug Abuse: Escape to Nowhere.* Philadelphia: Smith, Kline, and French Laboratories, 1967. Factual current information on drugs.

Amos, William E., and Jean Dresden Grambs, eds., *Counseling the Disadvantaged Youth.* Englewood Cliffs, N.J.: Prentice-Hall, Inc., 1968. The only book written on this topic. Essential reading for teachers and counselors working with disadvantaged populations.

Arbuckle, Dugald S., *Counseling: Philosophy, Theory and Practice.* Boston: Allyn & Bacon, Inc., 1965. Discusses the values of man and how they relate to the counselor in the chapter on theoretical issues.

Mowrer, O. Hobart, *The Crisis in Psychiatry and Religion.* Princeton, N.J., D. Van Nostrand Co., Inc., 1961. A collection of papers discussing ways in which religion and psychology can work together profitably. The author is critical of traditional psychonalysis for its failure to attend seriously to values.

Rubin, Isadore, and Lester A. Kirkendall, eds., *Sex in the Adolescent Years.* New York, Association Press, 1968. An unusually sound and honest discussion of the topic and its surrounding problems.

Sechrest, Carolyn A., *New Dimensions in Counseling Students.* New York: Teachers College, Bureau of Publications, Columbia University, 1958. Counseling presented through the analysis of verbatim cases. The case of Jackie is particularly helpful to understanding referrals.

10

Group Situations

Even though teachers can develop many opportunities
to counsel with individual students and parents, the
natural milieu of a teacher is a group situation. In
professional preparation for teaching much emphasis
is given to group discipline and group instruction.
When a teacher seeks a position, prospective employers
evaluate his ability in classroom management and in
preparing lessons for groups. They also inquire about
his skills in providing leadership for groups which
meet outside the school day, usually called co-curricular activities. He is expected to be able to handle
students in large groups, such as a lunchroom or assemblies. During his training a teacher may, of course,
hear a great deal about individual differences, but,
in general, he is supposed to give consideration to the
individual as a member of one of the multitudinous
school-determined groups. The school is organized so
that teachers seldom see students outside of some
group situation. Groups with which teachers deal differ in focus. Some center on the interaction of group
members, others center on content. To the extent that

a group is focused on the former, the teacher can find group counseling opportunities (See Chapter 2). As the group becomes more focused on content, counseling opportunities give way to instructional processes. Opportunities for group guidance occur when the primary focus of the content is with the personal concerns of the students. It becomes important for teachers to recognize the opportunities for implementing guidance and counseling goals in classrooms, large group meetings, and in co-curricular activities.

Group Characteristics

One must have some knowledge of the characteristics of groups before he can ascertain what goals might be implemented and how to go about it. A brief review of some of the current knowledge about group behavior is in order.

In speaking of a group, we are not talking about a mere assemblage of people. The occupants of a subway car do not compose a group. Neither do those students who for an hour or so dwell in an after school "detention hall." A group is an assemblage of people who have come together for a common purpose. The purpose may or may not be that which the organizers of the group intended. The group determines its own purpose and it may be either the accomplishment of some task or an involvement in its own dynamics. Most school groups are organized for task accomplishment. There is good rationale for having school groups which would be primarily concerned with interaction between members. Students could achieve considerable insight into their behavior and the quality of its effectiveness if schools offered more opportunity for the formation of groups where the primary concern would be an understanding of group dynamics. It is well for teachers to be aware of both possibilities.

Individuals bring their unique "selves" to a group. Teachers should be sensitive to the idiosyncratic qualities of each individual so that they will avoid considering pupils as stereotypes. An appreciation of the uniqueness of the individuals who make up any classroom was heightened for one of the authors by her participation in the following incident. At the first meeting of a university class in adolescent psychology, the instructor stepped to the podium. After a moment of silence, he said, "I am going to call the roll." He did this, and then remarked, "Calling the roll is something that every teacher in every classroom does.

Usually it is done just as I have done it. 'Sally Jones,' 'Present,' 'John Smith,' 'Present.' The next time you step in front of your class to call the roll, I challenge you to do it in a different manner. Do it like this: Call for the hungry. Who will answer? Call for the fearful and see who answers. Call for the angry, the timid, those who need love—call for all of these and when they answer you will know who really came to your class that morning!" The author has forgotten a good bit of the content of this course, but she remembers the lesson provided by this incident every time she begins a new class. The groups teachers work with are composed of living, breathing, reacting *individuals*, each one of whom is different. Each one behaves as best he can within the framework of his unique makeup and the situation where he is. Each one exhibits behavior which is reasonable to him.

A group is more than the individuals who compose it. Each group may be said to possess a personality all its own. It has characteristics which can be observed and described. A group has a flavor, morale, and cohesiveness. Teachers often express this concept when they compare their classes. "This is the best biology class I've ever had." or "I don't know what to do about my 4th period English. They are just not like the others." Teachers know that they never teach the same class twice.

Each group operates under some kind of leadership. The leadership may be overt or covert. There may be a difference between the appointed leader and the real leader. What teacher has not faced the experience of having a student threaten to unseat him? Leadership may be centered in one person or it may be shared among the members of the group. There are different styles of leadership. Sometimes they are classified as authoritarian, democratic, or laissez-faire. Often the leadership is a mixture of these types. The behavior and accomplishment of the group is relative to the type and quality of leadership which it receives. A teacher who is sensitive to his group provides for the kind of leadership needed. His style may vary as the situation varies. Just as groups are different because of the individuals who compose them, so individuals exhibit differing behavior in the various groups to which they belong. Teachers who are in a faculty meeting behave in a different way from when they are in the faculty lounge. The star athlete may exhibit great confidence in the locker room and just as great timidity at the awards banquet.

People are responsive not only to leadership but also to the type of position which they occupy in groups. Group positions in a classroom may be determined by the administration of an evaluative instrument called a *sociogram*. This device shows in graphic form those individuals who are popular with the group and those who are not. "Stars," i.e., those who are popular, react in a different manner from isolates or rejectees. A teacher who possesses a knowledge of the way in which the peers of a pupil appraise him is in a better position to understand behavior. The sociogram can be used not only to determine the attitude of the group toward its individual members but also to determine the degree and quality of relationships within the total group. A plotted sociogram can present a picture which looks like a chain. Here the tendency is for each student to choose a student who does not choose him. As this kind of picture indicates an immature group, the teacher who has such a class may want to furnish students with opportunities for a greater variety of relationships. Other sociograms indicate the presence of cliques. The teacher of such a group will be better able to deal with its inner relationships if he knows about groups involved. In still other classes, one student will receive an overwhelming majority of choices. This kind of situation will help the teacher know what qualities the group values in its leader. A sociogram of a mature group will indicate a variety of intricate relationships and may resemble a spider-web.

Group members respond not only to the kinds of groups in which they find themselves, and their positions in such groups, but also to group pressures for conformity to group standards. Individuals tend to act as they perceive other members of the group acting. Many individuals are reluctant to go against majority peer opinion. Literature on the psychology of adolescents is full of this concept, and it appears to extend into adulthood, as witness the "suburbia" syndrome and the behavior of "the organization man."

Knowledge about the behavior of groups is a discipline all its own, so we cannot hope to present an extensive study here. Our purpose is to bring to your attention some of the ideas which we think important as you work in your group situations. For further information, see the list of suggested readings at the end of this chapter.

Opportunities for Group Guidance

Since teachers work almost exclusively with groups, much of what they achieve by way of implementing guidance goals will take place in group settings. The goals, however, remain the same as those which are sought in working with individuals. Guidance in all its phases emphasizes assistance in the growth of each individual toward self-actualization. Guidance workers see their job as that of promoting the development of satisfying life goals. In order for the individual to accomplish this, he must have adequate self-knowledge, he must be able to make decisions and he must have the opportunity to test his decisions against reality. Teachers assist with these processes as they relate to their students in group situations. We will take a look at some of the groups with which teachers deal, with the idea of pointing out some of the opportunities. We, of course, cannot cover all situations, but perhaps a description of some may sensitize you to others which may be inherent in your own school classroom.

The Classroom   Teachers spend most of their occupational life in classrooms. Any person who visits a number of classrooms becomes aware that there are differences in the climates that pervade them. Some climates seem to be supportive of mental health. Some are just the opposite. What are some practices which promote healthy classroom climates, classrooms in which students may have a better chance to grow toward emotional maturity? We can look at a classroom which is likely to enhance mental health in terms of the physical surroundings and the teacher's attitude and behavior.

Classrooms which promote mental health are light, appropriately heated and ventilated, and colorful. They are clean, equipped with comfortable furniture and adequate instructional materials. Flexible seating and work space is provided and student work is displayed.

Teachers who promote mental health relate to students with respect and affection. They are warm, exhibit a sense of humor, are considerate of the individual and feel secure in knowledge of subject matter, methods of instruction and in relations with students. They make more positive responses than negative and look for something good in what a student does as well as give constructive criticism. These teachers like their subject-matter and they attempt to convince the student of its importance. They allow physical freedom of movement and encourage questions and the expression of differing points of view. They do not hesitate to set the limits necessary for a good working atmosphere. They are firm but kind, and they allow students to have some voice in what takes place. Teachers who promote mental health do not use methods of discipline which denigrate the student. The key to their behavior is that they *like* the people whom they teach. They accept each one as a worthwhile individual with unique potential and they communicate this attitude to their classes.

Before we leave the subject of the kind of climate conducive to mental health, it would be well to look at some other school practices which tend to promote just the opposite. These subtly affect the climate and may prevent even the best intentions of the teacher from being carried out.

One thing which increases the teacher's anxiety and subsequently makes him less able to work effectively in the classroom is that there is little place in some school systems for teacher failure and hence for innovation. Progress comes from creative experiment and one expects a certain number of failures before a successful outcome can be established. Industry knows this well and allows for it in the development of new products or processes. The school has yet to expect anything other than a positive outcome from an innovative procedure. Reluctance to subject human beings to experimental procedure is understandable. But ways must be found to test educational innovations if teachers are to develop better ways of teaching. It is unfair and unwise for the teacher who desires to experiment to be subjected to undue parental pressure and criticism. And yet it is the uncommon administrator who will encourage such practices. It is little wonder that teachers sometimes stifle their own creativity and, as a consequence, experience a sense of nonaccomplishment and frustration.

Another undesirable action of school systems is pressing students for achievement by means of threats: "If you don't make an 85 average you won't get into college." The school also tends to place, promote, and grade students by rigid and invalid standards. Students are placed in tracks by the use of test scores, they are promoted on the basis of achievement without regard to potential and they are given grades which are based on subjective and, often biased, opinion. In fact the very graded organization of the school, with its built-in arbitrary point of passing or failing, says to many a student, "Do the best you can and we will fail you." Many happenings or lack of happenings in the school are based on a sacrosanct schedule which makes the student and teacher serve it, rather than the other way around: "No changes in schedule will be permitted after September

15th." "You cannot take your section on a field trip. They might be late to the next class."

An undesirable classroom climate is engendered when teachers do not expect their students to learn. Negative expectations are indicated by common remarks such as, "Oh dear, I see we have another Robinson." "He's always been slow!" "Looks like a probable dropout to me." "Girls seldom do well in physics." Recent research indicates that teacher expectancy has a measurable influence on pupil achievement.[1] Teachers who expect less of Juan Sanchez than of John Smith may actually cause Juan to learn less than John. Indications are that when teachers expect certain children to show increased intellectual development, those children do just that. Teachers' expectations of student behavior seem to serve as a self-fulfilling prophecy. A teacher who is aware of the possible effect of his expectations and who desires to promote an atmosphere of mental health will maintain an optimistic attitude toward growth and achievement. He will not prejudge students on the basis of socioeconomic status, home conditions, ethnology, track placement, or test scores. He rather will maintain high expectations for the growth and development of each one. In order to accomplish this we may have to modify our viewpoint concerning the effect of past experience on behavior in the classroom. Many years ago, a wise supervisor attempted to increase a young teacher's awareness of the variety of experiences which children bring to the classroom. She said to the teacher, "You must remember that the children are not born on the steps of the school house." The teacher, now one of the authors, took the admonition to heart. It has helped her to understand children. But it also may have caused her to classify some children and expect less from them. In light of recent research it seems well for education to take a new look at practices such as testing, grouping, evaluating, and record keeping, which tend to shape teacher expectation. Perhaps, in some ways, it might be good to look at our students, at least in terms of our expectations, as if they had been born just outside our classroom door. Then the teacher might be less inclined to lower his expectations because of classifications and labels.

Finally, the school seldom recognizes the developmental stage of students in exercising sanctions. It tends to reward the conforming and punish those who try to exercise their individuality

[1]Lederer, Joseph, ed., "Institutionalization of Expectancy; A Special Issue" *The Urban Review*, Vol. 3, No. 1 (September, 1968).

even though the latter action might be essential to the accomplishment of a major developmental task. John is 14 and is trying to make his way with the girls. He thinks that he is unattractive and that girls never will like him. Consequently, he spends a good bit of time at the youth canteen and does not get his homework done. The school ignores John's need to make a satisfying heterosexual adjustment and fails him. This adds to his image of himself as an unsuccessful person. As John's teacher, what different steps might have been taken? If you were the sponsor of the teen canteen, what would you do?

All these practices effect the way in which teachers operate in the classroom. Such conditions make it hard for teachers to behave in ways which are beneficial to the mental health of their students. As an exercise you might like to think about other similar and detrimental school practices. What is the teacher's responsibility in these cases?

The Curriculum   An important aspect of an individual's growth toward self-realization is his perception of himself as a person who can succeed. A student's encounter with curriculum has much to do with the way in which he learns to perceive himself.

In making an attempt to describe opportunities for guidance and counseling which may be found in the curriculum, we are arbitrarily limiting our definition of the latter to course offerings. Teachers are responsible for teaching a certain amount of subject matter. Subject matter taught so that a student is successful in learning it, contributes to his positive concept of self. On the other hand, students, who are constantly faced with the failure of their efforts to learn, grow to think of themselves in negative terms. Regardless of the course, it would seem that if students have been compelled to enroll in it, then the school which compels has an obligation to provide opportunities for successful learning. Instead of the locus of standard being in the amount and degree of subject matter presented, it should be in the amount of opportunity for successful achievement presented to the learner.

A teacher's proficiency should be determined by his ability to stimulate learning rather than by the amount of subject matter covered. Teachers need to feel secure about starting with each student where he is and taking him as far as he can go. This should be the earmark of success, rather than trying to bring all children "up to standard."

It is not always easy for teachers to recognize opportunities for guidance inherent in their specific fields. It is important that such opportunities be pointed out because secondary teachers operate within a definitely prescribed curriculum.

Even though many educators may believe in a more flexible organization for the curriculum, the curriculums of present-day schools are primarily constructed according to grade levels in subject matter fields. Teachers of secondary schools are trained, certified, and employed according to the number of semester hours acquired in a subject. They are expected to cover certain portions of prescribed subject matter based on the level of the group of students assigned to them. Under these conditions, a realization of the opportunities for guidance present in his particular segment of the curriculum may be hard for a teacher to discern. For this reason, it is practical for us to consider some of the opportunities present in each division of the curriculum.

Vocational Information   One of the more obvious guidance opportunities which is prevalent in all subject matter areas is that of the dissemination of vocational information, information which is important in the vocational decision-making process. In some schools, guidance counselors have collected or developed guides to occupations which are related to subject-matter areas and resource units which can be used for classroom instruction. Following is an illustration of a resource unit which could be used in English classes:

Resource Unit

Subject—Related Vocations for English

1.   Career possibilities for those interested in English (level of ability indicated).*

> *Professional, semiprofessional, executive occupations*: editor, journalist, lawyer, judge, clergyman, reporter, executive secretary, teacher, professional or technical writer, author, actor, advertising expert, educational administrator, critic, publisher, research analyst, librarian, director of religious education, architect.

*This list is incomplete. It can be supplemented from the sources listed under Section 4, "Where To Get More Information."

Technical, clerical, supervisory occupations: insurance adjuster, correspondence clerk, employment interviewer, photoengraver, radio-TV announcer, printer, postmaster, salesman, stenographer.

Skilled technicians, clerical workmen: ticket agent, auctioneer, bookbinder, compositor, typesetter, engraver, floorwalker or supervisor, linotype operator, lithographer, printer, manager, salesman, typist, notary public, telephone operator, information clerk.

Semiskilled, unskilled occupations: messenger, office boy, copy boy, news vendor.

2. Training needed for careers in this area.†

Young people interested in professional, semiprofessional, executive occupations need: college graduation from a liberal arts college rated as a first-class institution; specialized training or experience in the skills of executive positions; the ability to do executive work; capacity and skills for efficient reading; travel experience or the benefits therefrom acquired by broad thorough reading.

Young people interested in technical, clerical, supervisory occupations need: high school, junior college, or technical school graduation; high average ability in language arts.

Young people interested in skilled technical jobs or lesser clerical jobs need: high school graduation; some generalized training beyond high school; average ability in expression of ideas, ability to give directions clearly, speech; skills in spelling, writing and the basic elements of grammar.

Young people interested in semiskilled and unskilled occupations need: completion of ninth grade; mastery of basic skills and some general abilities.

3. Employment outlook for English-related careers.‡

In general there will be a need for increased abilities and training at all levels in view of the fact that the working force of young people is constantly increasing. Jobs demanding less training and ability will tend to decrease. Service jobs will decrease in some areas due to technical

†The training suggestions are generalized. For more specific information, see Section 4.

‡For up-to-date employment outlook information, see the current *Occupational Outlook Handbook*.

advances and automation. In other areas unaffected by the above, service jobs can be expected to increase.

Demand for technical writers, librarians, educational TV workers and producers of mass fiction is expected to increase.

4. Where to get more information.

    Occupational Outlook Handbook. Washington, D.C.: U.S. Government Printing Office. Issued biannually.

    Dictionary of Occupational Titles. Washington, D.C.: U.S. Government Printing Office.

    Occupational files in counselors office and/or school library.

5. Points for discussion.

    While English as a subject provides definite career possibilities, it is also a subject which provides training in the skills of communication. Communication is a paramount concern in all fields of human activity. Skills in English are just as essential for the scientist and engineer as they are for the editor or lawyer. A director of admissions at a school of engineering states: "The person who is not crippled by a deficiency in communication is one of the select 50,000 destined to go far in his career."

    A survey of business and industrial concerns listed "lack of ability to write clearly and concisely and inability to speak effectively" as two of the major shortcomings of college graduates.

    Any occupation for which one needs college training requires English. This includes careers in math and science.

    College Board Scholastic Aptitude Tests for entrance to college demand verbal skills. The verbal score reflects one's vocabulary, ability to reason with words, comprehension in reading, extent of reading, and level of reading. Many colleges require 500 and above on this part of the test for entrance.

6. Other suggested activities.

    Ask students to recall incidents where some person's lack of ability in English gave the student an unfavorable impression.

    Students might like to interview a personnel manager

in order to find out what emphasis he places on skill in English when he hires employees.

Make a poster from help-wanted ads which illustrate possible jobs for persons with literary interests.

Interests determine the kinds of hobbies that people choose. Develop a list of hobbies that might result from literary interests. Which of these hobbies might lead to a vocation? Where in your school or locality can you find resources which would enable one to pursue these hobbies?

If you are seriously interested in any English-related career, make a complete job study of it. (An outline for a job study may be found in Robert Hoppock, *Occupational Information*, 2nd ed. [New York: McGraw-Hill Book Company, 1963] pp. 427–45.) Re-evaluate your interest after you complete the job study.

Read a biography or an autobiography related to the occupation in which you are interested. (For a fairly comprehensive list of early books see H. D. Kitson, *I Find My Vocation* (New York: McGraw-Hill Book Company, 1954.)

Your librarian can help you choose others.

Choose an occupation which interests you. Make a ladder showing the steps through which one must generally pass on his way to the top. Try to estimate the age at which you might attain each step. What experiences are available which might assist you in "trying out" this occupation? (Don't forget clubs, school activities, and courses.)

English teachers who are interested in providing vocational information will find this material helpful for use in individual conferences as discussed in Chapter 7 as well as for class presentations. Similar units for other subjects can be developed by teachers and counselors. An assignment of research papers on occupations related to a given field may be helpful to some students. Teachers who wish to develop a file of occupations for their own use or to do further research themselves in course-related occupations will find the guidance counselor a helpful resource. He can indicate additional places where information may be found and can show the teacher how to use the *Dictionary of Occupational Titles* for developing a comprehensive list of related occupations on various levels. In case the counselor is not available for such service, we recommend the following as

a comprehensive compilation of guidance information: Willa
Norris, F. R. Zeran and R. N. Hatch, *The Information Service
in Guidance.* 2nd ed. (Chicago: Rand McNally & Co., 1966). In
every course the teacher has an opportunity for broadening his
students' knowledge of occupations and thus affording them
better chances of making vocational choices which will be satisfactory.

Educational Information   In the same way teachers may be
helpful to students in providing information about the possibilities of post-high-school education in their respective fields.
Teachers can be readily available sources of information to
their students on prerequisites for study in particular fields as
well as resources on various phases of college life, including
social experience. Teachers may be the only college graduates
with whom some of our very able students come in contact. It is
difficult for many children to actually see themselves as college
students. This is especially true of children from lower socioeconomic families where there has been no college-experienced
adult to relate to. Sometimes this inability to develop an image
of himself as a college student causes an able student to fail to
prepare himself for further education. Teachers can help with
this difficulty by maintaining a sensitivity to the possibility of
the existence of the problem, by talking with the student about
higher education, and by consulting with the school counselor.

Individual Instruction   In all subjects it is becoming more possible for teachers to pay attention to individual requirements
for successful learning. As schools become more sophisticated
in the use of tests, teachers will have greater access to data
which will help them prescribe unique learning experiences to
be implemented through self-instructional materials. Learning
laboratories have been set up in which the student has access
to programmed instruction, self-help packets, cartridge film pro-
jectors, tapes and the like. The teacher who is concerned that
his students maintain the self-respect engendered by successful
performance will be mindful of opportunities which meet individual differences in need.

Guidance Opportunities in Content Areas   The very nature of
the subject matter in some areas of the curriculum provides
opportunities for guidance. Such opportunities are particularly

prevalent in classes where teachers work with individuals or small groups, and where the teacher becomes an active participant in group activity. We find these situations in Home and Family Life (Home Economics) classes, Fine and Industrial Arts, Physical Education, and Driver Education. It has been our experience that teachers of the above subjects tend to relate more often to individual students on a personal basis. Indeed, many teachers from these areas become interested in enrolling in counselor education courses because they have found such experiences so satisfying and because they want to learn to counsel more effectively with those who seek help from them.

Guidance in Subject Areas   Opportunities for guidance are not limited to the above subject-matter areas. *All* subjects contain opportunities for helping students with their social and emotional growth. Teachers can sensitize themselves to these opportunities. We are indebted to some of our teacher–students for helping us become aware of this. For several years we have taught a course called *Guidance in the Schools*. The students who take this course are teachers and intend to remain so. Their purpose is to develop an understanding of the ways in which they, as teachers, can contribute to the guidance needs of their students. We have had teachers of all secondary subjects in our classes. From them, we have learned about some of the specific opportunities which exist.

English teachers have used literature as a means of assisting their students with self-understanding. For some students the use of books relating to their particular problems has been similar to bibliotherapy. Some have used biographies and autobiographies in making vocational decisions. Many students have come to a better understanding of their adolescent years by the reading of such classics as J. D. Salinger's *Catcher in the Rye*, and Carson McCuller's *Member of the Wedding*. Creative writing can be a useful source of emotional expression, feeling, and desire. We have learned that the toughest guys in the school (when given the opportunity by a sensitive teacher) can become the most tender of poets. The writing of an autobiography (if the student trusts the teacher who is to read it) can provide the opportunity for a description of his self-concept and an expression of his hopes. Help in speech and participation in discussion can assist in the growth of self-confidence. The English teacher can use these ways and many others which he will find for himself if he has a real desire to help his students grow.

Teachers of mathematics and foreign languages face a common guidance problem in the secondary schools, as these subjects are generally used to differentiate between the college-bound and those who are not. It is indeed a dilemma for a teacher to have students assigned to Algebra II or French I who apparently do not have the ability to achieve in these areas. The sympathetic teacher realizes that it is no less a dilemma for the students. In such a case it may be well for the teacher and counselor to work with the student and his parents in order to help him achieve a more realistic appraisal of his potential and of alternate educational opportunities. It also seems to the authors that teachers in general should work toward making college entrance requirements more flexible and the possibility of changes in a student's schedule less rigid. Statements like this one, which is copied verbatim from a student handbook, "Changes in the student's high school program will not be honored after June 15th except for special reasons approved by the principal. Pupils are expected to continue throughout the year in the courses for which they register," have no place in an organization which is committed to optimum growth. Before we leave a consideration of guidance opportunities in mathematics and foreign language courses, we suggest that teachers of these courses make *every* effort to relate their subject to the practical, vocational, and cultural life of the student. It is apparent that in one way or another, all of tomorrow's citizens are going to have to acquire more facility with an understanding of mathematics than was necessary for their fathers. Similarly, citizens of the future must acquire more tolerance for different ways of living and different means of expression. In a world community we must learn to understand and communicate with each other. One language is no longer enough. Surely the teachers of foreign languages (and this includes English for many of our inner-city students) can help all students to acquire a facility at some level with a language other than their own and with it an understanding of another culture.

Teachers in the sciences and social studies also have unique guidance opportunities. All these fields offer new vocational opportunities which should be explored by students. The student's self-concept is highly related to the way in which he sees himself in relation to the biological and physical world. In developing his value system and his life goals, he needs to be aware of what man knows about life and the forces with which he has to deal. The social studies classes are replete with opportunities to discuss values, as the values and beliefs of other cultures and other times are studied. The student needs to wonder at the achievement of man in some areas and to chafe at his lack of achievement in others. To become a person, he must face ethical questions which advances in science pose and he must learn about how such questions have been and can be resolved. He needs to acquire more knowledge about himself, his anatomical and physiological reactions, his psychological and interpersonal behavior. He needs help in decision making and self-examination.

Perhaps in order for the teachers of physical and social sciences to be more effective in relation to the holistic development of the individual there should be more correlation between varying subject matter and more mutuality of goals. For example, as this material was being written, the press was full of news about the first successful heart transplants. The possibility of the transfer of organs from one human being to another is bound to have an effect on one's concept of self. It adds complexity to questions like "Who am I?" "What of me is actually mine?" "When do I cease to exist?" These are questions which the becoming person must resolve, and his resolution of them calls for concepts which are indigenous to the life, the physical, and the social sciences. Students (in their vocational and educational development as well as their personal social growth) require knowledge which is available only from teachers who have competency in the sciences. Content has optimum value to the student if it is taught by teachers who are concerned not only with the presentation of information, but with the impact which such knowledge can make on the student as a person.

Teachers of fine arts and industrial arts (and here we include the materials part of home economics), as well as teachers of physical education and driver education, have opportunities for helping students that are not as apparent in other subject fields. A person who is unsuccessful in highly academic fields may achieve greatly in areas where he uses his physical being either in transforming materials, in body activity, or in the skillful handling of objects. Art media, wood, metals, ceramics, textiles, and food all provide opportunities for creative manipulation by individuals who may be unable to achieve self-expression with less tangible material. The use of one's body in dramatics, dancing, games, and competitive sports affords a source of satisfaction which is not dependent on the cognitive demands of the more academic courses. Successfully learning to play a musical instrument, run a sewing machine, operate a band saw, or drive an automobile, all can contribute to the development of a healthy self-concept for all students but they are particularly important for students who have learned to think of themselves as retarded, failures, and nonachievers in other school experiences.

Conversely, teachers of these subjects should also be aware of the negative effects which students who are unsuccessful in these areas experience. The academically brilliant but athletically retarded student must suffer quite as much as his opposite when he is faced with the fact that he is, indeed, a nonachiever in physical education. Physical education teachers should be sensitive to the plight of such students and make provision for successful performance through special programs. Teachers of less academic subjects should attempt to derive a better fit between the individual's natural capacity and the tasks which are demanded from him. The awkward girl who finds the manipulation of material in sewing difficult should have special understanding and assistance from her home economics teacher. The boy who has difficulty in obtaining his driver's license needs sympathetic intervention from his teacher of driver education. The ultimate goal of these subjects as well as the others is the optimum development of the individual. Feelings of nonsuccess oppose such development.

In addition to subject matter which is fairly well defined by fields, there is knowledge which is vital to the personal development of students but which is in a gray area as far as assignment to a place in the curriculum. This area of knowledge consists of concepts in health, consumer education, child development and care, family life, sex education, and the like. Some of these essential concepts are taught in physical education, economics, psychology, or home economics. In earlier times, efforts were made in many secondary schools to have these ideas presented in "guidance classes" or in "homerooms." This is still being done in some places,[2] but the practice is no longer widespread. The authors are not experts in curriculum organization

[2] New York State Bureau of Guidance, *Group Guidance Programs*, Albany, N.Y.: New York State Board of Education, 1966.

and they do not presume to say where in the curriculum such subject matter should be placed. They do concur, however, that this is a vital part of the education of secondary school youth. It is self-evident that topics like these have a direct bearing on the psychosocial development of students and therefore such material should have a designated place in the curriculum. Much of this subject matter has an emotional concomitant. For this reason teachers who are given the responsibility for it should be exceptionally well-trained and extremely sensitive to its effect. Guidance opportunities in these areas are unlimited and it is here that the school counselor should be most closely associated with the teacher. It is here, also, that close cooperation between the school, the home, and other socializing agencies is most desirable. It goes without saying that every student does not need to be taught all the subjects which the secondary school curriculum provides. It is just as true that no student can become an adult, satisfactory to himself and to society, without gaining insight into the psychosocial areas which vitally affect his growth and behavior.

Teachers of subjects in which vocational skills are learned have an obvious guidance-related function in assisting their students with preparation for and placement in the world of work. Business, industrial arts, graphic arts, and home economics generally offer opportunities for learning salable skills to students who intend to terminate their education at the high school level. There are other opportunities for guidance in these classes which may not be as obvious as that of training for specific occupations. For example, there will be students taking these courses who should be encouraged to continue their education beyond high school. Others may need help in finding part-time jobs. Still others may be tempted to accept low-level employment and drop out of school. Teachers need to become involved in these decisions and to be especially alert to those students who are potential dropouts or in financial need. This is another crucial place at which teachers and school counselors should work closely together.

Large Groups

Most of the secondary teacher's time is spent with students in groups of classroom size. But he does deal with some large groups. He conducts study halls, monitors lunchrooms and is responsible for assemblies. In addition he encounters students at athletic events, school social events and performances. Participation in these groups provides opportunity for a teacher to observe his students outside the classroom setting. Such observations may make for better understanding. How does the student make use of his spare time? What are his procedures for studying? Is he usually with his gang at school functions and in the halls, or is he a loner? At what stage is he in his heterosexual development? What social skills does he exhibit or lack? A teacher who opens himself to what is going on can learn much about these and other questions.

As teachers participate in large groups, they have the opportunity to exhibit a spirit of friendliness toward students and to engage in informal encounters. Sometimes it may be necessary to reprimand a student. When this occurs, the teacher should try to do it with as little loss of face for the student as possible. It is not easy to censure behavior and still communicate a respect for the person, but it can be done. Reprimands given within this framework are generally more conducive to a student's growth than if this person is denigrated in the process.

Teachers who assume responsibility for student assemblies might consider guidance-related topics for programs. Vocational and educational information lends itself to this kind of presentation. The school counselor can suggest resources such as speakers, visual aids, and panels. At times it may be appropriate to invite former students to talk about their jobs, their experiences in the armed services, and in college.

Other topics of concern to young people such as smoking, the use of drugs, modern music, multimedia communications, hosteling, and the like may also be used. It is helpful to students to have them participate as much as possible in planning and carrying out programs. Audience participation is also desirable. Teachers should be able to help students use techniques like buzz groups, open forums, reaction groups, and role playing to stimulate discussion in larger groups. In using buzz groups, a large audience is divided into small groups of six or eight for discussion or the formulation of questions. At the end of a given period one member reports for his group to the entire audience. In the open forum approach, individuals in the audience are requested to respond to or question the speaker. If a large auditorium is being used, it is helpful to arrange microphones for the responses. Reaction groups are assigned specific listening tasks prior to the program; each group is expected to react to the assigned portion of the presentation. Role playing is an effective way to focus the attention of a large audience, and the effectiveness of this technique is increased if volunteers from the audience are used as role players.

Small Groups

Teachers contact small groups through committee work and co-curricular activities. In some classes, teachers may confer with committees which have been assigned special planning or research tasks. It is not unusual for committee assignments to be made in homerooms or for there to be meetings of the teacher with homeroom officers. Almost all secondary schools expect teachers to take part in some activity outside the classroom and this often takes the form of sponsoring a co-curricular group.

Guidance opportunities are found in small groups in two areas, interpersonal activity and content. As a teacher interacts with the members of a small group, he finds that he gets to know them better and in a somewhat different way from the classroom. He can help the members gain insight into how they tend to behave in a group and to make their behavior more effective. He sees that some students need encouragement toward greater participation, others need to learn to share participation, to keep quiet and listen. Some need practice in leadership, others in "followship." There are the silent ones, the aggressive, the rebellious, the verbose, the standard-keepers, the conforming, the doubting, the negative, the tension-reducers, the information-givers, and a host of others. Teachers who deal with small groups can help members look at themselves and can make it possible for them to help each other to more effective behavior. Such learnings are important, for much of the work of our society is accomplished in small groups. The adolescent who is helped to understand small-group behavior will be a more effective adult.

The purpose for which the small group was formed determines the content with which it deals. In our secondary schools we have groups formed for student government, social activities, special service, honors, and interests. The special interest may be related to a hobby or a vocation. In each group the adolescent has some opportunity to practice an adult role. He has a chance to test aspects of his self-concept against reality. If the group does not possess some autonomy and the group members some freedom of action, guidance opportunities are lessened.

Student government organizations possess limited authority delegated by the principal for formulating and administering rules under which students live. The organization is made up of elected members of the student body and is sometimes associated with a student court. Under the guidance of one or more of the faculty, members of the student organization participate in the process of democratic decision making, learn to abide by the limits of delegated authority, and learn to equate privileges with responsibility. Members grow in self-confidence as they act as representatives of their peers and as they adopt to a degree an adult role in government. They are often confronted with problems for which there are no easy or comfortable solutions. They are forced to evaluate their responsibilities in decision making. The faculty sponsor assists in the growth of the members by not allowing them to become dependent on adult intervention and by insisting that they make and accept responsibility for the decisions which are allowed them.

Social groups such as clubs (and in some secondary schools "sororities" and "fraternities") are generally formed spontaneously by the students themselves. The membership is usually self-selected. Sometimes the organization exists without the sanction of the school or faculty sponsorship. It is a controversial question as to whether the school should recognize these groups. It is a fact that they exist. If they are recognized by the school and sponsored by a teacher, he should have a keen understanding of the need of the adolescent to "belong." It may be well for a school which chooses to recognize social clubs to have enough of such organizations to provide a place for every student who cares to participate. Social clubs do have some positive aspects. They provide a means for peer relationship and a place for the adolescent to develop social skills. Under wise leadership, the members may learn to become more responsible in club activity, may adopt an altruistic purpose, and, in some measure, may exhibit growth in learning to tolerate differences. The same values can be achieved from membership in service clubs. This seems more in keeping with policy in a school which is democratically oriented. There is, however, a need for exclusiveness among adolescent groups. This need is so great that in some schools,

clubs which are ostensibly service-oriented in name and affilia-
tion become as exclusive regarding eligibility for membership
as those that are openly self-elected. Lack of belonging is a
severe burden to the unchosen adolescent, and this is a circum-
stance to which teachers and counselors must be especially sensitive. The assistance of meaningful adults can make a difference
in the way in which such a student sees himself and how he
copes with lack of acceptance by his peers. Artificial forced
acceptance or trying to make up the lack through contrived
events will not help. Making it possible for the student to gain
insight into his behavior and his values and purposes will help
him turn a defeating experience into one that is productive in
his growth as a person. The former course of action is just as
belittling to a student as is the rejection by his peers. The latter
course increases his strength and his dignity.

Honors groups are usually related to some form of school
achievement. They are based on competitive awards and the
intent is to inspire students to greater achievement. If this type
of motivation is to be used (and rightly or wrongly, it appears
to be inherent in our social structure) it would be well for
teachers to make sure that awards are not made for only one or
two forms of achievement. If outstanding success is recognized
in one field, then it should be recognized across the board. Thus
many students, rather than a select few, will have a chance to
view themselves in a favorable light—and individual differences
in type as well as amount of ability will receive recognition.

Clubs which are organized around vocational or avocational
interests usually open membership to any student who cares to
join. Teachers who sponsor groups which have compatible interests find the experience a rewarding one. Mutual interests
make genuine communication between generations more likely.
This kind of association makes for better understanding on the
part of both teachers and students. Hence, an adolescent has the
opportunity to relate to and perhaps emulate an adult who has
real skill in an admired sport or game or real knowledge about
a desirable hobby. In vocational clubs (such as Future Teachers,
Future Farmers, or Future Homemakers) the student becomes
involved with an adult who is a real professional in his field.
Such contacts made in an atmosphere of friendliness and mutual
interest affect the adolescent's image of himself in a positive
way.

Parent Groups

One other type of school-related group with which teachers deal is composed of parents. The existence of such groups is not as extensive in secondary schools as in earlier years. Nor do secondary schools deal as directly with groups of parents as do their elementary counterparts. But when secondary teachers do have the opportunity for such meetings, there is much implication for guidance. It is a cultural phenomenon for adolescents to disassociate themselves from their parents during the secondary school years. However, the schools may be losing an opportunity for making the break less severe on both generations by not affording parents more contact with their children's education. Parents receive little chance to develop an understanding of the kind of education that the school is trying to provide and even less chance to discover what their adolescent children need from them.

Teachers can seek out places in the curriculum where there might be appropriate encounters between parents and children. One instance that immediately comes to mind is in the area of family living. It has been demonstrated that parents can join skillfully led discussion groups and talk with their children about common concerns. When this kind of discussion is organized and conducted by the schools, it seems to engender a less threatening or embarrassing situation than might exist if the discussion took place at home.

Other opportunities for the involvement of parents might come about in cooperation with community agencies. As an example, in Prince Georges County, Maryland, the Mental Health Association sponsors a weekly FAMCHAT. The letters stand for "Fathers and Mothers Converse Here About Teenagers." It would spoil the acronym but shouldn't the teachers be in on this, also?

SUMMARY

Many opportunities for guidance and counseling are inherent in the groups with which teachers work. In order to capitalize on these opportunities teachers must know about the characteristics of group behavior. They need to be aware of classroom practices which promote mental health and those which do not. Each subject field in the curriculum has content which, if taught with this purpose in mind, can increase a student's confidence in himself, add to his positive concept of self, and aid him in determining and achieving satisfying life goals.

The teacher is not limited to classroom groups in his efforts to provide guidance for his students. He can also utilize opportunities found in large-group activities and in smaller co-curricular groups. Finally, the teacher should be aware of the opportunities to further the socioemotional growth of students by working with groups of parents.

The teacher who is a successful guidance worker in group situations has certain commitments. He is committed to the total development of his students. He is aware of the opportunities which groups present for the encouragement of such development and is sensitive to the unique needs and possibilities of each of the group members. The same qualities which contribute to effective counseling with individual students contribute to positive relationships in the classroom and successful work with informal groups.

SUGGESTED READINGS

Bennett, Margaret E., *Guidance in Groups*. New York: McGraw-Hill Book Company, 1963.
The subtitle of this book is "A Resource Book for Teachers, Counselors, and Administrators." It is just that and a good one.

Fedder, Ruth, *Guidance in the Homeroom*. New York: Teachers College Press, 1967.
A description of how teachers and counselors can analyze the homeroom in order to understand it and the individuals who are influenced by it.

Fedder, Ruth, *Guidance Through Club Activities*. New York: Teachers College Press, 1965.
The author describes actual club groups as they were used for the guidance of club members over a period of time.

Garry, Ralph, *Guidance Techniques for Elementary Teachers*. Columbus, Ohio: Charles E. Merrill Books, Inc., 1963.
This book is devoted primarily to the elementary teacher. However, pages 389–99 contain information on the con-

struction and interpretation of sociograms which is applicable to any situation.

Glanz, Edward C., *Groups in Guidance*. Boston: Allyn & Bacon, Inc., 1962.
Glanz relates groups to guidance and education. He describes the dimensions of groups and presents ways in which group theory and techniques can be used in guidance activities.

Gazda, George M., and Jonell H. Folds, *Group Guidance: A Critical Incident Approach*. Chicago: Follett Educational Corp., 1968.
A manual of lesson plans which include references and aids for students and leaders.

Gronlund, Norman Edward, *Sociometry in the Classroom*. New York: Harper & Row, Publishers, 1959.
This is a comprehensive and somewhat technical reference. It is recommended for those who wish to supplement the above information.

Hoffman, Randall W., and Robert Plutchik. *Small-Group Discussion in Orientation and Teaching*. New York: G. P. Putnam's Sons, 1959.
Although this book is focused on college freshman orientation classes, it is a good reference for any teacher who is interested in small-group leadership in the classroom.

Kemp, C. Gratton, *Perspectives on the Group Process*. Boston: Houghton Mifflin Company, 1964.
Selected readings on the group process from the fields of education, psychology, sociology, and philosophy. This book will provide the reader with a better understanding of interdisciplinary contributions to knowledge about small-group behavior.

Lifton, Walter M., *Working With Groups*, 2nd ed. New York: John Wiley & Sons, Inc., 1966.
A very helpful resource for increasing understanding of the relationship of group action to contemporary social issues. Also included are many suggestions for the application of group techniques in educational settings.

Waters, Jane, *Group Guidance*. New York: McGraw-Hill Book Company, 1960.
A resource of great practical value to the secondary teacher. Group techniques are clearly described and school group work in various situations is thoroughly discussed.

11

The Teacher Who Counsels

Is the teacher who counsels any different from the teacher who sees little of individual students? In this final chapter, the characteristics and attitudes of teachers who counsel are considered. In discussing these characteristics and attitudes, we turn to experience and those studies which have tried to assess the characteristics of successful counselors.[1] Counseling is, and may always be, more of an art than a science and thus only partially open to empirical evaluation.

Three major criteria for evaluation are (1) the attitudes which the teacher has toward students; (2) the goals of the teacher; and (3) the extent to which the teacher possesses personal characteristics which contribute to good counseling.

[1] For example:

C. B. Traux, "Effective Ingredients in Psychotherapy," *Journal of Counseling Psychology*, Vol. 10 (Fall, 1963), 356–63.

Fred E. Fiedler, "The Concept of an Ideal Therapeutic Relationship," *Journal of Consulting Psychology*, Vol. 14 (August, 1950), 239–45.

Jerome C. Brams, "Counselor Characteristics and Effective Communication in Counseling," *Journal of Counseling Psychology*, Vol. 8 (Spring, 1961), 25–30.

Feelings about Students

Teachers cannot establish a counseling relationship unless they have a positive attitude toward students. They can neither alienate themselves from students nor become sentimentally attached to them. Rather, they must support each student in his struggle for identity and create opportunities for his growth toward becoming the individual that only he can become.

The attitude toward students which teachers who can effectively counsel must have can be clarified by comparing it with undesirable attitudes. One undesirable attitude is that of ignoring personal and social needs of students and of concentrating solely on subject-matter. Teachers who demonstrate this attitude in the extreme are unwilling or unable to establish effective processes with students, that is, to meet them at all on the level of feeling. Their exclusive concern is the transmission of didactic knowledge.

To such teachers, the adolescent student is, at best, a sponge-like absorber of subject-matter. The worth of the student is directly proportional to his achievement in learning what the teacher hands down and much woe is visited upon those students who cannot or will not respond to the teacher's presentations. Such teachers desire to instruct perfectly homogeneous groups, preferably of superior academic ability. Teachers who fall in this first category are concerned only with intellectual achievement. They either ignore the affective domain or they consider affective needs of students the business of socializing agencies other than the school. Teachers who are unwilling or unable to establish affective processes with students cannot counsel. Fortunately, they do not want to.

Another undesirable attitude is that of sentimental fondness toward students. Teachers who possess this attitude in the extreme profess to love all adolescents all of the time. They vacillate between condescending amusement and trying to be one of the group. They make great efforts to be popular with their students, often by behaving more like a teenager than an adult. Because our society is a youth-centered one, sentimental fondness for students may be interpreted as sincere concern. School officials may be guilty of this erroneous interpretation and give counseling duties to teachers on no other basis than their professed fondness for students. A teacher whose attitude toward students is based primarily on sentimentality may lack sincerity. He overreacts to adolescent moods and sometimes becomes a victim of them. Adolescents do not usually respond warmly to this kind of teacher, but they are not above taking advantage of him in gaining privileges and liberties for which they may not be ready or which may not be appropriate within the school situation. For example, they may encourage the teacher to permit such a jolly atmosphere in the classroom that no learning takes place.

Unfortunately, many teachers who are sentimentally fond of students desire to act as counselors. They see themselves as counselors in a pleasant buddy-buddy relationship with students but they are unaware of the extent to which the counseling relationship calls for limits and for the acceptance of unpleasant feelings such as hostility. Their counseling activity should be discouraged.

What kind of attitude toward students is held by teachers who have the will and the capacity to establish a relationship with students which is based on acceptance, understanding, love, and respect—the same qualities which were described in Chapter 2 as essential to a good counseling relationship? Such teachers see students as worthwhile persons who are engaged in the very important, difficult, and exciting task of becoming adults. A teacher who has this point of view understands the struggle which confronts a student as he makes his way through his developmental tasks toward adulthood. Such a teacher appreciates both the despairs and the joys of adolescence. He knows that an adolescent's behavior is neither unimportant nor superficial to the adolescent. For example, what appears to be puppy love to the adult is real to the adolescent and part of his development toward adulthood. An adolescent's behavior has profound meaning both for him and for those around him whose own achievement toward adulthood enables them to help adolescents on their way.

Understanding of this kind on the part of a teacher engenders love and respect for a fellow human who is striving for fulfillment and identity. Because of his own struggle toward maturity, this teacher knows that the adolescent cannot achieve maturity by having the road always smoothed for him. He has the wisdom not only to teach needed academic skills but to help the student experience learnings which will enable him to become a satisfactory and satisfying (to him) adult. He seldom feels the need to talk about his love for students. He rather indicates his love by providing experiences which allow for full emotional expression, by allowing the student an appropriate degree of autonomy even to the extent of occasional failure, and by maintaining attitudes of sensitivity, encouragement, and honest appraisal. He is the steadying, the beckoning hand, never the one that delivers harsh blows or condescending pats. As a teacher and as a person, he is able to communicate cognitively and affectively with his adolescent students. "Effective teaching involves a two-way communication process. Not only must the student understand what the teacher is saying, and meaning, but the teacher must understand what the children are saying and meaning."[2]

A teacher who can establish relationships with students based on the above attitudes can and should counsel.

Goals as a Teacher

The ultimate goals of a teacher have bearing on whether he can counsel. Each of us who is a professional educator must face a question of purpose. "For *what* am I here?" "Why am I teaching this material to these students?" It is not enough to reply, "Because it is in the curriculum." Typical answers to these questions are apt to be framed in words which, from overuse, have lost much of their meaning. But finding a reply satisfactory to himself is a task which a teacher who desires to counsel cannot shirk.

For what are *you* teaching? What are *your* goals? We invite you to dismiss jargon, forget your textbooks, clear your head of what others have said, think about the questions just asked, and state your answers in as few and as simple words as possible. With your own goals clearly in mind, you are free to read the authors' statement of goals which seem to them consistent with the practice of counseling.

A teacher who counsels has as his ultimate goal, as the end product of his efforts, students who have become adults who are satisfying to themselves and to a democratic society. Boy and Pine begin their book by saying,

> There is an emerging professional awareness that, when teachers and counselors are involved in the process of

[2]Rodney A. Clark and Wolcott H. Beatty, "Conceptual Framework for Teacher Education," *Mental Health and Teacher Education* (The Association for Student Teaching, 46th Yearbook, 1967), p. 61.

assisting youngsters, both groups are working toward common professional goals that revolve around one central goal: the total well-being and development of the individual.[3]

The school, that agency of socialization within which teachers work, is only one of many agencies of socialization and so the teacher must delineate his area of responsibility in affecting the development of the individual. In so doing, he must realize that although many socializing institutions may affect the individual, the school is the only one which exerts influence over *all* the children of *all* the parents. This fact means that the school and its teachers occupy a unique place in the process of socialization.

In essence, the school, and the school alone of all agencies, has responsibility for every child in the nation. Schools, which have so widespread an influence, must have important business. What *is* the business of the school? It is, of course, valuable to know what other people have said about this. But it is more worthwhile, if you are to counsel, to come to your own conclusions about where the school's (and therefore your) responsibility lies in helping your adolescent students become adults. Bloom's taxonomy of educational objectives is helpful in considering the responsibilities of the school and yourself.[4] He describes three domains of educational endeavor: *cognitive, affective*, and *psychomotor*. The cognitive domain deals with the "recall or recognition of knowledge and the development of intellectual abilities and skills." The affective domain deals with "changes in interest, attitudes, and values, and the development of appreciations and adequate adjustment." The psychomotor domain is "the manipulative or motor-skill area." If we adopt the viewpoint that the objectives of the schools can be classified in this way, then we must decide what objectives are to be emphasized and where and how they are to be implemented.

It would be hard to find a high school whose *stated* objectives do not incorporate equally both the cognitive and affective domains. On the other hand, it would be just as hard to find a school which is organized and managed so that both domains receive equal emphasis in the educational process. Most effort in most schools is directed toward cognitive objectives. A look

---

[3]Angelo V. Boy and Gerald J. Pine, *The Counselor in the Schools* (Boston: Houghton Mifflin Company, 1968), p. 3.

[4]Benjamin S. Bloom, ed., *Taxonomy of Educational Objectives: Handbook I: Cognitive Domain* (New York: David McKay Co., Inc., 1956), p. 7.

at the processes of evaluation in the high schools will support this statement. Students are grouped, graded, and promoted primarily on the basis of recall of knowledge and achievement in intellectual skills. Rewards are in terms of academic progress and are not given for achievement in the development of interests, appreciations, or values. Not only students but schools themselves are evaluated in the same way. In rating schools the predominant criteria are associated with academic performance often determined by standardized test scores.

To say that schools do not give sufficient attention to affective objectives in no way subtracts from the importance of cognitive objectives. We only wish to emphasize that educators must be just as concerned with objectives in the affective domain as in the cognitive domain. Any teacher who counsels must be committed to affective learnings as equally important.

A teacher who counsels must feel a responsibility for the total development of his students; he cannot be content with prescribed curriculums and techniques which deal only with cognitive objectives. Teaching for affective objectives is difficult, which is one reason why these objectives are so often ignored in practice. Bloom states that objectives in this domain are not clearly stated, that teachers are uncertain as to what learning experiences promote the attainment of the objectives, and that it is difficult to describe the behaviors appropriate to these objectives.[5] Nonetheless, the teacher who is committed to helping his students become all that they can become must accept the challenge of finding better ways of helping their total growth, which is dependent on learnings in the affective as well as the cognitive domain. Counseling and guidance practices certainly provide one source of departure.

The teacher who counsels, then, recognizes his business and the school's as that of providing experiences for students that will enable them to grow into satisfactory and satisfying adults. The teacher who recognizes that the experiences he provides students must promote both cognitive and affective objectives is encouraged to consider counseling as one avenue toward his goal.

Personal Characteristics

Interaction between people in a helping relationship can either facilitate or retard personal development of the person being

[5]Bloom, *Cognitive Domain*, p. 7.

helped. Carkhuff and Berenson point to extensive evidence that this is so:

> There is extensive evidence to indicate that, to a large degree, the facilitative or retarding effects can be accounted for by a core of dimensions which are shared by all interactive human processes, independent of theoretical orientation; that is, patients, clients, students, and children of persons functioning at high levels of these dimensions improve on a variety of improvement criteria, while persons offering low levels of these dimensions deteriorate on indexes of change or gain.[6]

These dimensions are listed as empathic understanding, positive regard, genuineness, and concreteness of expression. Almost the same characteristics of effective counseling relationships are described in Chapter 2 of this book as empathy, positive regard, congruence, and unconditional positive regard.

The question for the teacher who counsels is: "What kind of person do I need to be to develop a facilitative helping relationship with my students?" What personal characteristics contribute to a person being genuine, congruent, empathic, etc.? What is it that makes a person able to accept and reach out to different kinds of people, to welcome new experiences, be open and genuine in his relationships with others, and willing to be closely involved with others?

At one level the answer lies in the area of values and beliefs, such as respect for the worth and dignity of each individual, and for the right of the individual to work out his own destiny and belief in his capacity to so do. If values and beliefs of this kind are to be translated into effective human relationships, then they must be internalized, that is, become so much a part of a person that they can determine his behavior without his having to think about them. Belief in the worth and dignity of each individual is constantly verbalized in our society while at the same time it is being denied on all sides by housing and employment restrictions based on race, sex, or age in spite of laws forbidding them; unequal educational opportunities; irrelevant curriculums; school rules which enforce conformity; etc. This kind of conflict between belief and behavior becomes impossible to the extent that the person internalizes his beliefs. For the per-

---

[6]Robert R. Carkhuff and Bernard G. Berenson, *Beyond Counseling and Therapy* (New York: Holt, Rinehart & Winston, Inc., 1967), p. 4.

son who wants to be effective in interpersonal relationship, beliefs about the worth of each individual must be internalized to give him the strength to resist the pressures in school and society that are inimical to the individual.

At a deeper level the answer lies in self-understanding and self-acceptance. A person who sees little worth in himself is unable to see worth in others. A person who does not like or accept himself finds it difficult to like or accept others. Brammer and Shostrom refer to studies which support this view and point out that the ". . . significance of these findings for a counselor is that he must accept himself before he can accept his clients sufficiently well to help them."[7]

Knowledge and competence are also needed. These too are possessed by the kind of person who can function effectively in interpersonal relationships. The teacher who counsels needs to know as much as possible about different cultures, societal problems, issues in education, individual behavior, and adolescent development. This knowledge can help him understand and more easily accept himself as well as various kinds of students and their behavior.

Becoming a Teacher Who Can Counsel

How does one become an emotionally mature person who can be an effective teacher and counselor? Is it possible to change and become more genuine, more empathic, more caring, more loving, more acceptant? We think it is, in part by taking courses and studying and in part by being open to a variety of out-of-school experiences. Course work and study contribute to increased knowledge and competence. Intellectual understanding is essential but clearly not enough. Colleges, just like secondary schools, devote most of their energies to cognitive objectives. Those who are teaching or preparing to teach, and who wish to work toward affective objectives in their own lives, must ordinarily look elsewhere than in the academic world. (Some teacher education programs, however, are beginning to incorporate group counseling, sensitivity training, and similar activities into their curriculum.)[8]

[7]Lawrence M. Brammer and Everett L. Shostrom, *Therapeutic Psychology*, 2nd ed. (Englewood Cliffs, N.J.: Prentice-Hall, Inc. 1968), p. 176.

[8]*Mental Health and Teacher Education* (The Association for Student Teaching, 46th Yearbook, 1967).

Personal Therapy   Some people feel that all teachers would benefit from therapy, that those who are working with children should have as much understanding of themselves as possible. No one of us has completely realized his potential for emotional growth. A counselor (whether he be a psychiatrist, clinical psychologist, minister, or some other professionally recognized counselor) can help us remove roadblocks in the way. The experience of being counseled contributes not only to emotional growth but also to an understanding of what it is like to come to a person for counseling. Teachers who have engaged in personal therapy give their view that ". . . a teacher who has become more thoughtful in dealing with the affairs of his own life can be more thoughtful in his relations with students and colleagues."[9] They felt more able to examine their own feelings aroused during teaching, more sure of what they wanted to do, and more able to enjoy their work. Although they found that more students came to them for help, they were more aware of the limits within which teachers can counsel.

Teachers who wish to find out about possibilities for therapy can consult mental health clinics for local resources.

Sensitivity Training   Sensitivity training is a technique which aims to increase a person's self-awareness, his sensitivity to others, and his knowledge of how others react to him. It is an intensive group experience in which group members think, talk, and share feelings together in order to realize new psychological insights and to increase their awareness of and sensitivity to themselves and what goes on around them. Garwood finds that the benefits of sensitivity training include

> . . . recognition of psychological blind spots; improved solutions to specific interpersonal problems at work and in the family; steps in fundamental personality growth comparable to those sought in insight-oriented psychotherapy; decreased alienation, increased psychological accessibility, and closer, more communicative relationships with spouses.[10]

[9]Arthur J. Jersild and Eve Allina Lazark, *The Meaning of Psychotherapy in the Teacher's Life and Work* (New York: Bureau of Publications, Teachers College, Columbia University, 1962), p. 115.

[10]Dorothy Seminow Garwood, "The Significance and Dynamics of Sensitivity Training Programs," *International Journal of Group Psychotherapy*, Vol. 27, No. 4 (October, 1967), 461.

Brammer and Shostrom refer to "Self-Actualization Groups" with dual emphasis on academic instruction and group experience.[11] Although sensitivity training is a technique of long standing, it is just now becoming popular and easily available. School districts are utilizing it to help teachers increase their self-understanding and hence their effectiveness in working with students. Sensitivity groups (or encounter groups, or marathon groups, or T groups, or self-actualization groups) are increasingly available in many communities. Involvement in such groups when directed by well trained leaders offers teachers considerable possibility for personal growth.

Information about opportunities for sensitivity training, self-actualization groups, or encounter groups may be had from the Esalen Institute, Big Sur, California, or from the National Training Laboratory, National Education Association, Washington, D.C.[12]

Literature   Those who counsel should know and assimilate as much of the human experience as possible. Naturally all human experience cannot be known directly by any one person. One turns, therefore, to the vicarious experiences provided by authors, actors, and other artists. That those experiences are valid is supported by a study by Riley and Standley. This study

> . . . suggests agreement between the imaginative insights of writers and the experimental investigations of therapists. In fiction and drama, positive human interactions were distinguishable from negative encounters on the basis of conditions believed to be crucial in counseling and psychotherapy. Literature and counseling provide mutually supporting descriptions of constructive human relationships.[13]

Literature is rich in fiction and drama which contribute to a broader understanding of the human condition and adolescence

[11]Lawrence M. Brammer and Everett L. Shostrom, *Therapeutic Psychology*, 2nd ed. (Englewood Cliffs, N.J.: Prentice-Hall, Inc., 1968), pp. 322–23.

[12]For a fuller description of sensitivity training, see William C. Shutz, *Joy, Expanding Human Awareness* (New York: Grove Press, 1967).

[13]John E. Riley and Fred L. Standley, "Literature and Counseling: The Experience of Encounter," *Counselor Education and Supervision* Vol. 7, No. 4 (Summer, 1968), 328–34.

in particular.[14] In identifying with the characters portrayed in the literature, the reader comes to understand some of the feelings and behaviors of different kinds of people. A broad range of reading for teachers can be both profitable and enjoyable.[15]

Leisure-Time Activities   A person can also broaden his emotional spectrum by participation in one or more satisfying leisure-time activities. Such experiences provide increased enjoyment if they are shared with others, though there is a place too for solitary activities which give you time for quiet and solitude. Adults need to play, to create, to have fun. Many local recreation programs, "Y's," religious organizations, and adult education programs give opportunity to pursue old interests and pick up new ones.

Being with Different People   It is somewhat difficult to find opportunities for forming relationships with people who are different from ourselves. Our social structure encourages association between similar people. One must generally make a deliberate effort to cross social and ethnic lines for really meaningful relationships. The effort is essential, however, if one is to be an effective teacher and counselor of adolescents. A teacher or counselor must be willing to undergo some discomfort as he seeks to relate to people who have a different way of life. He can expect to encounter, if not prejudice and rebuff, at least a feeling of not being a part of the group. He can also expect to acquire an increased understanding for and appreciation of human differences and an added richness to his life.

Real acceptance of the worth of every individual is seldom found. It is also rare to find a real commitment to the fact that everyone does not have to be like oneself or a real belief in the right to differ. These are goals worth striving for if one is to be a teacher who counsels and who understands the "generation

14For a listing of novels which may help bridge the "generation gap" between adolescents and adults see Alma C. Spithill, "The Valuable Allies" *Personal and Guidance Journal*, Vol. 46, No. 9 (May, 1968), 879–83 or N. Tasker Witham, *The Adolescent in the American Novel* (New York: Ungar, 1964).

15There are many books written for the lay public which can be very helpful in understanding different people and different cultures. A few examples are: Eldridge Cleaver, *Soul on Ice* (New York: McGraw-Hill Book Company, 1968). William H. Cobbs and Price A. Grier, *Black Rage* (New York: Basic Books, Inc., Publishers, 1968). Oscar H. Lewis, *La Vida* (New York: Random House, Inc., 1966).

gap" (the wide differences between adolescents and adults) and the wide differences among adolescents. The more we are able to form satisfying relationships with differing fellow men, the closer we come to these goals.

A teacher can strive for these kinds of interpersonal relationships by travel, by belonging to cross-cultural organizations, by offering friendship to colleagues who belong to another group, by visiting neighborhoods which are unlike his own, and by working with social action groups such as those concerned with civil rights and liberties. Participation in sensitivity training groups can also expose one to different kinds of people.

Everyday Contacts   This last experience seems almost too obvious to be discussed, yet it is an area which is often overlooked. If we desire to improve our communication skills, we do not stop practicing them when we leave the school. Instead we try to utilize *all* our contacts with others to increase our ability to communicate on a level "beneath-the-surface." We listen to the beautician. We are interested in the checkout girl at the supermarket. We try to increase our understanding of the postman and the doctor.

A person who wishes to counsel communicates his feeling for people in his everyday life. He is sad when they are sad and he rejoices with them when they are happy. He learns to experience the feelings of other people and to communicate to them that he does so. As he relates to other people in his daily contacts, he practices the art of his trade. He listens and he feels. He learns respect and tolerance for differences. He communicates understanding and love.

SUMMARY

The teacher who counsels has attitudes toward students based on acceptance, understanding, love, and respect. He is clear about his goals as a teacher, goals which go beyond immediate classroom goals to take in the total development of each individual student. He possesses personal characteristics similar to those of effective counselors and those of people in general who engage in helping relationships. Brammer and Shostrom point out that the counseling relationship though in some ways unique has similarities to other human situations such as the teacher-pupil situation. "In one sense," they say, "a counseling relationship is an extension of ordinary, yet healthy, living processes."[16] This extension is what the teacher who counsels works toward.

To work toward being an emotionally mature person who can counsel effectively with the students who come to his classroom, the teacher can engage in personal therapy and sensitivity training, turn to leisure-time activities and literature, and broaden and deepen his contacts with different kinds of people. He can be as open to as many experiences as possible, not only accepting those that come but looking for new ones.

The world today, though exciting in many ways, is also confusing and frightening to both adolescents and adults. It is easy to feel a sense of impotence, a feeling that there is nothing one can do to change situations which one believes are damaging to people. Students in high schools and colleges complain too of anonymity, that no one knows them. Much of current unrest in high schools comes from feelings of impotence and anonymity. Students want to know that they count for something. They need a sense of personal awareness to which teachers can contribute by recognizing them as individuals. Glasser writes:

> Equally important to having responsible adults talk with students in school is giving students the chance to express their ideas to the adults who have control over their lives in school. In most meetings of school boards, faculties, and parents with teachers, students should be included and asked for their opinions. Our failure to maintain a dialogue with students sows the seeds for our current campus disruptions, which are attempts by students to get adults to listen.[17]

Adolescents need adult help in growing up in this world. Teachers who believe that they can make a difference and who are able to enter into helping relationships with their students can give adolescents some of the support, courage, and personal awareness they need.

It is a revolutionary world which we live in, and this generation at home and around the world has had thrust

[16]Brammer and Shostrom, *Therapeutic Psychology*, p. 161.
[17]William Glasser, *Schools Without Failure* (New York: Harper & Row, Publishers, 1969) p. 223.

upon it a greater burden of responsibility than any generation that has ever lived. Some believe there is nothing one man or one woman can do against the enormous array of the world's ills. Yet many of the world's great movements of thought and action have flowed from the work of a single man.[18]

SUGGESTED READINGS

Allport, Gordon W., *Becoming.* New Haven, Conn., Yale University Press, 1955.
Theory of personality which repudiates a narrow mechanistic concept of man. Describes man as continually changing and ceaselessly bestirring himself in the pursuit of objectives that are never fully attained.

Frankl, Viktor E., *Man's Search for Meaning.* New York: Washington Square Press Inc., 1963.
A confirmation of man's ability to transcend conditions of extreme emotional deprivation. Based on the author's experience in concentration camps and his personal search for meaning.

Fromm, Erich, *The Art of Loving.* New York, Harper & Row, Publishers, 1956.
Required reading for anyone who wishes to understand more about what love is.

Jersild, Arthur T., *When Teachers Face Themselves.* New York, Teachers College Press, 1955.
Teachers talk about their fears, joys, hopes, anxieties, and frustrations in their life and work as teachers. The importance of self-understanding on the part of teachers is made very clear.

Krathwohl, David R., Benjamin S. Bloom, and Bertram B. Masia, *Taxonomy of Educational Objectives, The Classification of Educational Goals, Handbook II: Affective Domain.* New York: David McKay Co., Inc., 1964.
Describes the nature of the affective domain and its classification structure.

Moustakes, Clark E., *The Authentic Teacher.* Cambridge, Mass.: Howard A. Doyle Publishing Company, 1966.

[18]Quoted from Robert F. Kennedy in Edward M. Kennedy, "A Tribute to his Brother," *Vital Speeches of the Day,* Vol. 34, No. 18 (July, 1968), 546–47.

The experience of teachers who attempted to foster emotional growth in themselves and in their pupils.

Overstreet, Harry, and Barnes Overstreet, *The Mind Alive.* New York: W. W. Norton & Company, Inc., 1954.
Describes mental health and suggests means for achieving emotional well-being.

Rogers, Carl R., *On Becoming A Person.* Boston: Houghton-Mifflin Company, 1961.
Writing for lay as well as professional people, Rogers shares his experiences as a person and a therapist with the hope the book can help with personal living. It is a very personal kind of book.

Tillich, Paul, *The Courage To Be.* New Haven, Conn.: Yale University Press, 1952.
The thinking of theologians, both modern and ancient, can help in developing our values and searching for meaning. This book can add to understanding of ourselves and the human condition.

Index